True Tales™
of
Freezing Land

Henry Billings
Melissa Stone Billings

STECK-VAUGHN
ELEMENTARY · SECONDARY · ADULT · LIBRARY

A Harcourt Company

www.steck-vaughn.com

Acknowledgments

Editorial Director: Stephanie Muller
Senior Editor: Kristy Schulz
Associate Director of Design: Cynthia Ellis
Design Manager: Alexandra Corona
Production Coordinator: Rebecca Gonzales
Media Researcher: Claudette Landry
Page/Cover Production Artist: Dina Bahan

Cartography: Pp. 4–5, 7, 15, 23, 31, 39, 47, 55, 63, 71, 79, 87, 95, MapQuest.com, Inc.
Illustration Credits: Pp. 13, 21, 37, 45, 53, 61, 69, 85, 93, 101, Eulala Conner
Photo Credits: Cover (background) ©Superstock; (inset) ©Galen Rowell/CORBIS;
Back cover (inset) ©AP/Wide World Photos; p.1 ©Superstock; p.3 ©Corel Photo
Studios; p.6 ©Phil Schermeister/Corbis; p.8 ©Superstock; p.9 ©Mark
Gallup/Uniphoto; p.10 ©No Limits Photo, ©Mark Wellman; pp.14, 18 Courtesy
Starkist Foods, Inc.; p.17 ©James Kay/Uniphoto; p.16 ©Llewellyn/Uniphoto;
p.22 ©Galen Rowell/CORBIS; pp.24, 25, 26 ©Canada Press; pp.30, 32 ©Corbis;
p.33 ©PhotoDisc; p.34 ©Mark DuFrene/Contra Costa Times; pp.38, 42 ©AP/Wide
World Photos; p.40 ©Steve Berman/Liaison Agency, Inc.; p.41 (both) ©AP/Wide
World Photos; p.46 ©Crandall/The Image Works; p.48 ©Phil Schermeister/Corbis;
p.49 ©Galen Rowell/CORBIS; p.50 ©Jonathan Blair/CORBIS; p.54 ©Stone;
p.56 ©Corbis; pp.57, 58 ©Dexter Filkins/Los Angeles Times; p.62 ©Superstock;
pp.64, 65, 66 ©JIM LEO/The Herald; pp.70, 72 ©AP/Wide World Photos;
p.73 ©Viennareport/SIPA Press; p.74 ©AP/Wide World Photos; pp.78, 80, 81, 82
©Newspix; p.86 ©Galen Rowell/CORBIS; pp.88, 89, 90 ©AP/Wide World Photos;
p.94, 96, 97 ©Superstock; p.98 ©Ralph Barrera/The Austin American Statesman;
p.108a ©NOAA; p.108b ©Superstock; p.108c ©B. Osborne/Earth Scenes;
p.109a ©Galen Rowell/Corbis; p.109b ©Stone; p.109c ©Corbis.

ISBN 0-7398-2393-0

Contents

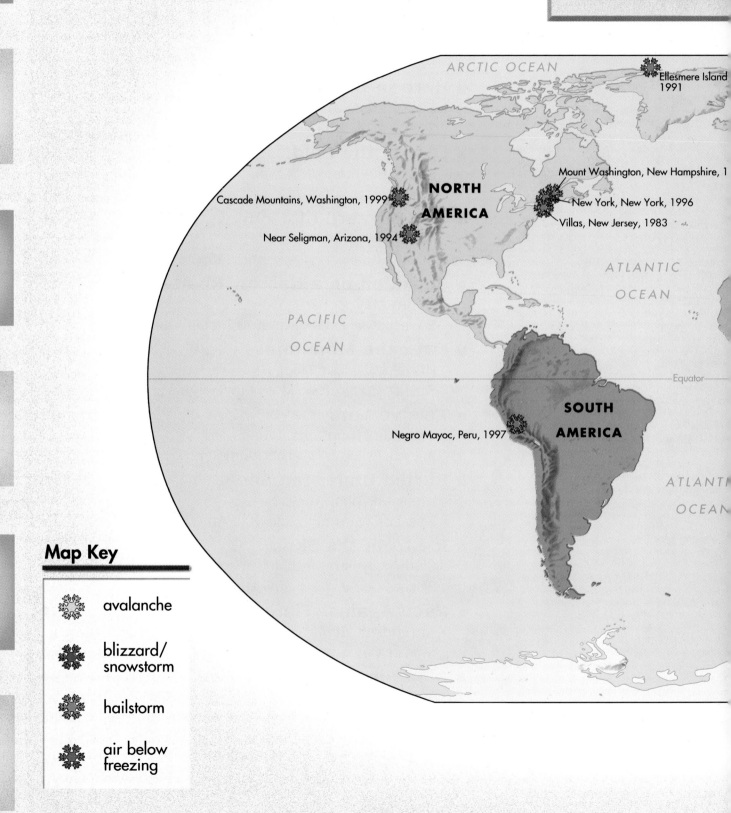

ARCTIC OCEAN

Ellesmere Island
1991

NORTH
AMERICA

Cascade Mountains, Washington, 1999

Mount Washington, New Hampshire, 1

New York, New York, 1996

Villas, New Jersey, 1983

Near Seligman, Arizona, 1994

ATLANTIC

OCEAN

PACIFIC

OCEAN

Equator

SOUTH
AMERICA

Negro Mayoc, Peru, 1997

ATLANTI

OCEAN

Map Key

❄	avalanche
❄	blizzard/ snowstorm
❄	hailstorm
❄	air below freezing

4

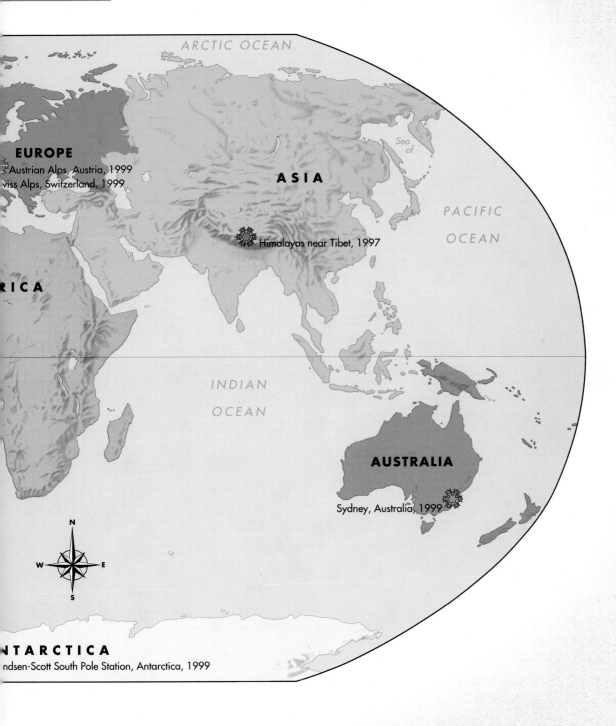

f

and

ARCTIC OCEAN

EUROPE
Austrian Alps, Austria, 1999
viss Alps, Switzerland, 1999

ASIA

Sea of

PACIFIC

OCEAN

RICA

Himalayas near Tibet, 1997

INDIAN

OCEAN

AUSTRALIA

Sydney, Australia, 1999

N

W   E

S

NTARCTICA
ndsen-Scott South Pole Station, Antarctica, 1999

Trapped on the Mountain

Hugh Herr was only 17 years old. Even so, he was one of the best rock climbers in the world. He knew how to make his way up all sorts of mountains. Herr was also very good at ice climbing. He could climb up walls of rock even when they were covered with ice.

On January 23, 1982, Herr decided to go ice climbing with a friend named Jeffrey Batzer. They headed up Mount Washington in New Hampshire. The day began well. But it didn't end that way.

Lost on the Mountain

As Herr and Batzer got closer to the top of the mountain, it began to snow. So they faced a choice. They could turn back or they could take a chance and try to climb to the top. They decided to keep going up. Herr said later, it was "one bad decision."

Mount Washington is 6,288 feet high. That is not very high for a mountain. Many mountains are two or three times as high. Still, Mount Washington can be a very dangerous place. Over the years, many people have died there. One reason for that is the weather. Mount Washington has some of the worst weather in the world. Storms can begin very quickly there. It can be sunny one minute and stormy the next.

Herr and Batzer soon found out about the quickly changing weather. As they headed toward the top of Mount Washington, strong winds began to blow. The winds became a storm. Then the storm turned into a **blizzard**. This storm had winds of driving snow blowing more than 32 miles an hour. Suddenly, the two men could barely see each other. They were caught in a **whiteout**. The snow was very heavy. It was so thick that everything looked white.

Herr and Batzer decided to turn around and head down the mountain. As they did, the blizzard blew stronger and stronger. Soon the winds blew at 70 miles an hour. The two men hurried down the trail. They hoped to return the way they had come. But in the blinding snow, they **wandered** off the trail into the woods. The freezing **temperature** and the high winds made them very cold. By then, the **wind-chill factor** had dropped far below zero. As the two men walked through the woods, the snow was often up to their chests.

At one point, Herr and Batzer followed a frozen stream. But the ice was thin. The ice broke, and the men fell through. Then they were wet and very cold. "I felt **incredible** fear," said Herr later.

When night came, Herr and Batzer dug a hole under a large rock. They put some pine branches in the hole. They sat together in the hole, trying to keep warm.

Weather can change suddenly over a mountain.

An avalanche swept over Albert Dow while he searched for the two men.

Pain and Death

The next day the two men continued down the mountain. Herr began to see bridges and trails that weren't really there. By the end of the day, he and Batzer were still lost. They slept out in the open for the second night. By January 25, their legs were weak and frozen. That made it hard to walk. They could take only a few steps before falling down.

Meanwhile, people had begun to search for them. One of these people was 28-year-old Albert Dow. Like Herr, Dow loved climbing. He was willing to do whatever he could to help a fellow climber in trouble. Sadly, Dow's climbing skills couldn't save him on this day. As he made his way up the mountain, a huge **avalanche** swept over him. This tumbling river of snow killed him.

Climbing Again

By January 26, Herr and Batzer had given up all hope of living. So the two men sat down and waited for death to come. That afternoon, a woman named Cam Bradshaw was **snowshoeing** on the mountain. She saw footprints in the snow. The prints seemed to be going in circles. To Bradshaw, that was a sure sign that someone was in trouble. She followed the prints until she came to Herr and Batzer lying against a rock. They were still alive but barely.

Bradshaw called for help. Soon a helicopter arrived and took Herr and Batzer to the hospital. There, doctors had to remove five of Batzer's toes and his left foot. They also had to take off parts of four fingers and a thumb. Being out in the cold for so long had caused great **damage** to these body parts.

Herr was in even worse shape. His legs had been badly damaged when they froze. For two months, doctors tried to save his legs. But it was no use. At last, the doctors removed both of Herr's legs six inches below the knees.

Doctors told Herr he would never climb again. But he did not believe that. He got a pair of **artificial** legs. Then he began to build up his strength. It took months of hard work. But by 1986, Hugh Herr was again one of the best ice climbers and rock climbers in the world.

Hugh Herr

Read and Remember — Choose the Answer

❋ Draw a circle around the correct answer.

1. What did Hugh Herr like to do?

   ski   go ice climbing   study weather

2. What did Herr and Batzer do when it started to snow?

   called for help   kept climbing up   set up camp

3. What did Albert Dow do?

   went skating   joined the search party   headed home

4. Where did Herr and Batzer spend the first night?

   in a hole   in a cabin   in the open

5. Who found Herr and Batzer?

   Albert Dow   doctors   Cam Bradshaw

Think About It — Drawing Conclusions

❋ Write one or more sentences to answer each question.

1. Why do you think people climb Mount Washington? _____

   _____

2. What made Herr and Batzer wander off the trail? _____

   _____

3. Why did Herr and Batzer give up all hope of living? _____

   _____

4. Why did Cam Bradshaw follow the footprints in the snow?

   _____

   _____

Focus on Vocabulary — Find the Meaning

❄ Read each sentence. Circle the best meaning for the word or words in dark print.

1. The **blizzard** moved in quickly.

rockslide   bad snowstorm   mudslide

2. Herr and Batzer were caught in a **whiteout**.

thick, blowing snow   fog   rainstorm

3. The two men **wandered** off the trail.

tried to slide   walked away from   crawled

4. The **temperature** dropped.

snow pile   water level   level of heat

5. The **wind-chill factor** was very low.

how cold the air feels   wind speed   ice level

6. He felt **incredible** fear.

tiring   amazing   freezing

7. A huge **avalanche** began.

search party   rushing snow   growing fear

8. She was **snowshoeing**.

walking on snow with special shoes   fishing   hunting

9. The cold caused great **damage**.

harm   changes   excitement

10. Herr climbed with **artificial** legs.

heavy cloth   very sharp   made by people

How Snow Forms

Sometimes **water vapor** collects on tiny bits of dust in clouds. If the air in the cloud is freezing, tiny ice **crystals** can form. All ice crystals have six sides. When the ice crystals stick together, they can make flakes of snow. Study the diagram below. Write the answer to each question.

Water vapor collects on tiny bits of dust.

Ice crystals form if the air in the cloud is freezing.

Ice crystals stick together and make snowflakes.

If the outside air is 32°F or colder, heavier snowflakes can fall to the ground.

1. What collects on tiny bits of dust? _____

2. What can happen if the air in the cloud is freezing? _____

_____

3. How many sides do ice crystals have? _____

4. How are flakes of snow made? _____

_____

5. What temperature must the air outside the cloud be for snow to fall? _____

A Dog to the Rescue

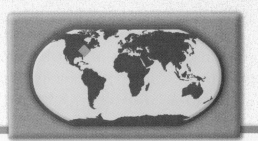

There was no school on February 11, 1983. It was snowing too hard in the town of Villas, New Jersey. Still, 11-year-old Andrea Anderson asked her mother if she could play outside. Bea Anderson said she could. But she warned Andrea to stay close to the house.

Andrea went out with her two sisters, Heather and Diane. Before long, the sisters got cold. They went back inside. Andrea stayed out to play by herself. She had no idea that in a few moments she would be fighting for her life.

All Alone

Andrea didn't realize just how bad the storm was becoming. Later, people would call it the "blizzard of 1983." The storm's wind blew stronger and stronger. Soon it was blowing 60 miles an hour. The wind blew the snow all around. The blowing snow made it hard to see. The **visibility** dropped to almost zero. That meant it was almost impossible to see farther than a few feet.

Outside in the wind and snow, Andrea got cold. Like her sisters, she decided to go inside. But as she started toward the house, a powerful **gust** of wind knocked her off her feet. The wind blew her 40 feet from the house. It sent her tumbling over the edge of a **snowbank**.

At the very bottom of the snowbank was a large **snowdrift**. This deep pile of snow had been formed by the wind. As the wind swept over the flat ground, it left some spots bare. It covered other spots with extra snow.

The snowdrift that Andrea landed in was so deep that she couldn't climb out. She tried. But each time, she slipped back. She grew colder and colder. She also grew scared. Andrea screamed for help. But no one heard her. The roar of the wind blocked out her loud cries.

Luckily, a dog named Villa was outside at the time. Villa was a one-year-old dog. She belonged to Andrea's neighbors, Dick and Lynda Veit. Andrea often played with Villa. Andrea even helped take care of Villa when the Veits were away.

Villa heard Andrea's screams. She sensed that the girl was in trouble. Quickly, Villa leaped over the fence around the yard. Then she dashed through the deep snow. She slid down the snowbank and found Andrea stuck in snow up to her chest.

A Special Dog

Villa licked Andrea's face. That warmed the girl's cheeks a little. Then Villa began walking in circles around Andrea. At first, Andrea didn't know what the dog was doing. But soon it became clear. Villa was

The blizzard made it hard to see.

The wind can blow snow into large snowdrifts.

using her big paws to pack down the snow. She was getting ready to pull Andrea out of the snowdrift.

Soon the dog stopped walking. She stood next to Andrea without moving. Andrea understood what Villa wanted. She put her arms around the dog's strong neck. She held on tight as Villa began pulling her forward.

Slowly, the 100-pound dog dragged the girl out of the deep snow. When they reached a bare spot, Andrea stood up. She didn't have much strength left. She was **shivering** with cold and fear. Her hands and feet were **numb**. So she just grabbed the fur on the back of Villa's neck. She hoped the dog would lead her to safety.

After a moment, Villa began moving forward again. She pushed her way through the snow to the top of the snowbank. But then a gust of wind knocked Andrea down. Villa rushed over to her and stretched out her neck. She waited for Andrea to grab on again. Time after time, the wind blew Andrea to the ground. Each time, Villa was there to pull her to her feet.

Back Home

After 15 minutes, Villa and Andrea finally reached the Anderson house. By then, Andrea was **exhausted**. Villa pulled her onto the porch. Then the dog scratched on the door to get help.

Inside the house, Bea Anderson had seen a shadow on the porch. Then she heard the scratching. As she went to the door, she looked at the clock. She was surprised to see that half an hour had passed since Heather and Diane had come inside.

When Bea opened the door, Villa had **disappeared**. She had returned to her home. But Andrea was there, weak and cold. "Mom," Andrea cried, "Villa just saved my life."

It was true. Andrea would have died if she had stayed in the snowdrift much longer. The **combination** of cold air, deep snow, and high winds would have killed her. The wind-chill factor during the blizzard was well below zero. Only Villa's quick **rescue** had saved Andrea Anderson from certain death.

Villa's owner was very proud that her dog had saved Andrea's life.

USE WHAT YOU KNOW

Read and Remember — Finish the Sentence

❋ **Circle the best ending for each sentence.**

1. Andrea Anderson asked her mother if she could _____.
  walk the dog   play outside   stay home alone

2. Andrea was knocked off her feet by the _____.
  cold   dog   wind

3. To get to Andrea, Villa had to jump over _____.
  a fence   a wide hole   a pile of rocks

4. Villa dragged Andrea out of the _____.
  car   snow   house

5. Andrea held onto Villa's _____.
  leash   neck   tail

6. Villa brought Andrea to her _____.
  car   house   school

Write About It

❋ **Imagine that you are Andrea Anderson. Write a paragraph explaining why you think Villa is a hero.**

_____

_____

_____

_____

_____

_____

USE WHAT YOU KNOW

Focus on Vocabulary — Match Up

Match each word with its meaning. Darken the circle beside the correct answer.

1. visibility
   ○ sound ○ distance something can be seen ○ stillness

2. gust
   ○ sudden burst of wind ○ cold water ○ bit of dirt

3. snowbank
   ○ hill of snow ○ river of snow ○ hole in snow

4. snowdrift
   ○ snow shovel ○ pile of snow made by wind ○ trail

5. shivering
   ○ climbing ○ screaming ○ shaking

6. numb
   ○ without color ○ without feeling ○ without sound

7. exhausted
   ○ sleepy ○ exited ○ very tired

8. disappeared
   ○ fell down ○ jumped high ○ went out of sight

9. combination
   ○ tools ○ mixture ○ pieces

10. rescue
    ○ act of saving someone ○ thoughts ○ movement

20

Seasons

Earth spins on an imaginary line called an **axis**. The axis is **tilted**. This makes parts of Earth lean closer to the sun. Earth also moves around the sun. The sun shines more on the parts of Earth that are closest to it. This causes changing **seasons**. Study the diagram. Write the answer to each question.

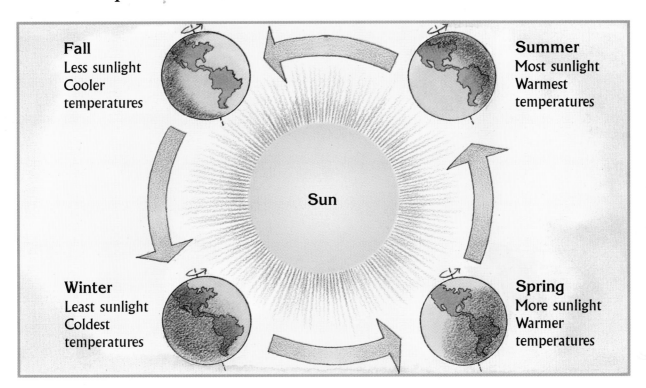

Fall
Less sunlight
Cooler
temperatures

Summer
Most sunlight
Warmest
temperatures

Sun

Winter
Least sunlight
Coldest
temperatures

Spring
More sunlight
Warmer
temperatures

1. What are the four seasons? _____

2. What is an axis? _____

3. During which season does an area get the most sunlight?

_____

4. Which season gets the coldest temperatures? _____

5. Does an area get more sunlight in spring or in fall? _____

Hero in the Frozen Arctic

Pilot John Couch had flown in all kinds of weather. He had flown through wind and rain. He had flown across hot **deserts**. But, on October 29, 1991, he was flying to one of the coldest spots in the world. Couch was a pilot in the Canadian army. He and four crew members were taking 14 people to the tip of Ellesmere Island in northern Canada. That meant flying over the Arctic Ocean, almost to the **North Pole**. The land there was covered with ice and snow. The wind and cold made it a very dangerous place.

In the Cold

Couch was not worried about the cold. He and his passengers were warm inside the plane. It was dark as they headed for the island's airport. But that was not surprising. During that time of year, Ellesmere Island got only two hours of sunlight a day.

When the plane was 35 miles from the airport, Couch got ready for the landing. But then something went wrong. Suddenly, the plane began to drop very quickly.

"We're going to crash!" yelled one of the 14 passengers. Couch did his best to control the army airplane. But there wasn't much he could do. The plane crashed nine miles from the airport. It bounced along the **tundra** for almost a mile. Then it came to a stop on the frozen ground.

People rushed to get out of the plane. Couch was trapped in the plane along with crew member Joe Bales for a short while. The two men were not badly hurt. But they had a hard time getting free.

Joe Bales, at right, was a crew member on the plane.

Finally, they pushed their way out of a window. Just after they got out of the crashed plane, it burst into flames.

Couch and Bales stood together for a moment as the plane burned. Then they began looking around. They found 14 people still alive. Ten were badly hurt. But it was not the **injuries** that worried Couch. It was the terrible cold. The temperature was four **degrees** below zero. The wind made it feel even colder. Couch knew they had to do something fast or they would all die.

Helping Others

The fire burned most of the things on the plane. But Couch managed to save a few sleeping bags. He helped people climb into them. That made the **survivors** a little warmer. Couch then gave up his own hat, gloves, and coat to others. It was a very brave thing to do. It meant that Couch himself was in greater danger of freezing to death.

Couch gathered most of the survivors together out of the wind. He made the survivors stay near the only part of the plane that had not burned. This was the tail, or back, of the plane. But two people were so badly hurt they could not be moved. One of these people was Sue Hillier. As she lay on the snow, Couch walked over to her. "I'm not going to leave you," he said.

Couch built a wall of snow around Hillier to keep her out of the wind. He did the same for the other person who couldn't move. Then he made a small fire with **debris** from the plane. All night he stayed with these two people. Couch talked to them and kept their hopes up. He told them that they would be rescued soon. "I'll never forget his voice," Hillier said. "He saved my life."

A Brave Man

The survivors had hoped that a rescue plane would come soon. But a blizzard swept in, making a rescue impossible. Icy snow fell from the dark sky. The wind blew more than 40 miles an hour. There was no way that any plane could fly in such bad weather.

The blizzard lasted for two days. During that time, Couch did his best to keep everyone alive. He made

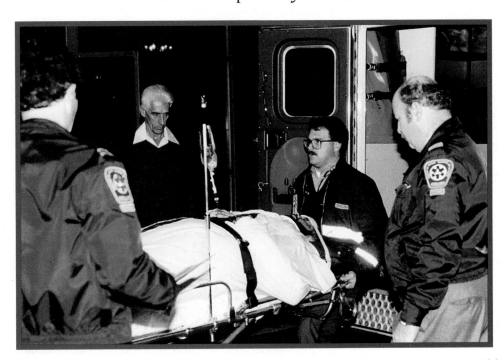

Rescuers rushed the survivors to hospitals in Canada.

sure that people took turns lying in the warmest parts of the plane's tail area. He didn't let them fall into a deep sleep. He knew that if they did, their body temperature would drop more quickly. Then they would freeze to death.

Even with Couch helping them, the survivors **suffered** terribly. Some had burns from the fire. Many were cut and bleeding. Some also had broken bones and other injuries. But most of all, they were terribly cold. At times, the wind-chill factor dropped to 76 degrees below zero. **Frostbite** set in. That meant that people's hands, toes, and faces began to freeze.

At last, on the morning of November 1, rescuers reached the area of the crash. They found 13 people still alive. Only one person had frozen to death. That person was John Couch. Joe Bales said that Couch "fought right to the end." But without warm clothes, he couldn't stay warm enough. He died just a few hours before rescuers arrived.

Those who made it out alive knew they owed their lives to Couch's brave actions. "There are 13 people alive because of the **efforts** of John Couch," said survivor Paul West. "It's because of him that we're here today."

The survivors talk about their struggle to stay alive after the plane crashed.

Read and Remember — Check the Events

Place a check in front of the three sentences that tell what happened in the story.

_____ **1.** John Couch's plane crashed into a lake.

_____ **2.** Ten people were badly hurt in the crash.

_____ **3.** Couch did his best to keep everyone alive.

_____ **4.** Sue Hillier walked to get help.

_____ **5.** A blizzard kept rescue planes away for two days.

_____ **6.** John Couch was the only one who did not die.

Think About It — Fact or Opinion

A **fact** is a true statement. An **opinion** is a statement that tells what a person thinks. Write **F** beside each statement that is a fact. Write **O** beside each statement that is an opinion.

_____ **1.** Ellesmere Island is in northern Canada in the Arctic Ocean.

_____ **2.** It is better to be too hot than too cold.

_____ **3.** John Couch was not badly hurt in the crash.

_____ **4.** A fire burned most of the things on the plane.

_____ **5.** Couch did not want people to fall asleep.

_____ **6.** Sue Hillier was the luckiest one of all.

_____ **7.** People's hands, toes, and faces began to freeze.

_____ **8.** John Couch should not have given up his coat.

USE WHAT YOU KNOW

Focus on Vocabulary — Crossword Puzzle

Use the clues to complete the puzzle. Choose from the words in dark print.

deserts   **North Pole**   **suffered**   **efforts**   **frostbite**

injuries   **survivors**   **degrees**   **tundra**   **debris**

Across
3. when part of the body freezes
6. units used to measure heat
8. harm to parts of the body
9. dry areas of land that get little rain
10. felt pain

Down
1. hard work to get something done
2. point on Earth that is farthest north
4. frozen land with no trees
5. broken parts of something
7. people who stayed alive

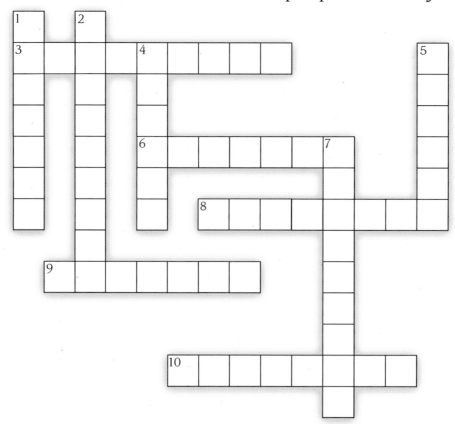

Wind-Chill Chart

❄ When it is windy outside, the air feels much colder than the actual **temperature**. This is called **wind chill**. For example, if the air temperature is 0°F and wind speed is 10 miles per hour, the wind-chill temperature is –22°F. Study the chart below. Circle the answer to each question.

Wind-Chill Chart

Wind Speed (in miles per hour)	Air Temperature (in °F)					
	30°	20°	10°	0°	–10°	–20°
0 mph	30°	20°	10°	0°	–10°	–20°
10 mph	16°	3°	–9°	–22°	–34°	–46°
20 mph	4°	–10°	–24°	–39°	–53°	–67°
30 mph	–2°	–18°	–33°	–49°	–64°	–79°
40 mph	–5°	–21°	–37°	–53°	–69°	–84°

1. What does *mph* stand for?

degrees   miles per hour   number of feet

2. If the wind speed is 0 miles per hour, how does the air feel?

colder   warmer   same as actual air temperature

3. If the wind speed is 10 miles per hour and the air temperature is 20°F, what is the wind-chill temperature?

–22°F   –34°F   3°F

4. If the wind speed is 20 miles per hour and the air temperature is –10°F, what is the wind-chill temperature?

–24°F   –53°F   –10°F

Lost in the Cold

It had been a long trip. Annabelle and Vinson Goodwin had driven all the way from California to Arkansas. There, the elderly couple had visited with friends. Then, on November 13, 1994, they were on their way back to California again.

Vinson was at the wheel. He steered the couple's blue camper van west through the high hills of northern Arizona. Driving on highway I-40, the Goodwins passed through the town of Seligman. Then they began the lonely 70-mile drive to Kingman. They hadn't gone far when they ran into trouble.

A Wrong Turn

The Goodwins didn't know it, but a storm was moving into the area. The **forecast** called for snow and wind. Back in Arkansas, the temperature had been about 60 degrees. It was even that warm in southern Arizona. But it was much colder in northern Arizona. The **elevation** was much higher. In fact, the Goodwins were more than a mile above **sea level**. There, snow often fell as early as November.

Twenty-five miles past Seligman, the Goodwins ran out of gas. As their van rolled to a stop, they wondered what to do. Neither Vinson nor Annabelle was dressed for cold weather. So they decided to wait in their van until someone came along to help.

Luckily, a police officer soon came by. He gave the Goodwins a small amount of gas. He told them to drive to the next exit and turn around. Then they should head back to Seligman to fill up their tank.

The Goodwins drove to the next exit. But then Vinson Goodwin made a wrong turn. He headed away from Seligman. So the Goodwins ended up on a road that went out into the snowy **wilderness**.

Within minutes, the road turned to dirt. Vinson tried to find his way back to the highway. He took one turn after another. But these roads were not marked in any way. So there was no way to tell which one to take. The only people who usually used the roads were hunters and farmers.

As the Goodwins tried to find their way back to the highway, a **snowstorm** moved in. The air filled with snow. That made it hard to see. Soon the Goodwins were completely lost.

Four Miles Away

Before long, the van rolled to a stop. The small amount of gas given to them by the police officer was gone. This time there was no one around to help. Again, the Goodwins waited in their van and hoped that someone would come. Finally, two hunters came by. The hunters stopped and gave Vinson Goodwin **directions** to the highway. Then they headed deeper into the wilderness.

It begins to snow in northern Arizona as early as November.

The van was lost in the snowy wilderness.

Vinson Goodwin learned that the highway was four miles away. That didn't sound too far. So Vinson decided to walk there and get help. Annabelle agreed to stay in the van and wait for his return.

When Vinson Goodwin left the parked van, he was wearing sneakers, jeans, a light coat, and a cap. That was not much **protection** against the cold, snowy air. It wouldn't take long for the cold to work its way through his thin clothing. Still, Vinson thought he could make it to the highway before he got too cold.

A Long Wait

Annabelle Goodwin watched her husband walk off into the snowstorm. Then she settled back in her seat to wait. As the hours passed, snow built up on the windows of the van. Annabelle grew cold, so she wrapped herself in a blanket. Late that afternoon, the hunters passed by on their way home. They offered her a ride. But Annabelle didn't want to be gone when her husband returned. So she turned them down.

For two long weeks, Annabelle waited in the cold van. There was fruit, bread, and cold meat there.

She ate this food a little at a time to make it last. She sang, slept, and tried to stay warm. Another snowstorm came and dumped even more snow on the area. Outside, everything was white and **frosty**. Still, Annabelle hoped her husband would return.

At last, on November 28, another hunter came along. He found Annabelle cold and exhausted but alive. She was rushed to a hospital. Meanwhile, a search party was sent out to look for Vinson.

As it turned out, Vinson Goodwin never reached the highway. He walked just half a mile before the cold air **chilled** him. His body temperature dropped. He became confused. Leaving the road, he wandered off into thick bushes. Rescuers found his body lying in four inches of snow. Vinson Goodwin died of **exposure**. Being out in the cold, wind, and snow had killed him.

Annabelle Goodwin knew she was lucky to be alive. She, too, could have died. But somehow she had made it through two weeks of snow and cold. "She's a very strong person," her daughter later said. "She's a fighter."

Vinson Goodwin's family will miss him greatly.

Read and Remember — Choose the Answer

❄ **Draw a circle around the correct answer.**

1. Why did the Goodwins stop on highway I-40?

They met friends.　　　They hit ice.　　　They ran out of gas.

2. What did the police officer give them?

a speeding ticket　　　a small amount of gas　　　a map

3. What happened when Vinson Goodwin took a wrong turn?

The van crashed.　　　They got lost.　　　They got a flat.

4. Who did the Goodwins see while they were lost?

two hunters　　　a young boy　　　wild animals

5. What did Annabelle Goodwin do?

She talked.　　　She stayed in the van.　　　She cooked.

6. How long did Annabelle Goodwin wait?

two hours　　　two weeks　　　two months

Write About It

❄ **Imagine you are a newspaper reporter. Write three questions you would like to ask Annabelle Goodwin.**

1. _____

_____

2. _____

_____

3. _____

_____

Focus on Vocabulary — Finish the Paragraphs

Use the words in dark print to complete the paragraphs. Reread the paragraphs to be sure they make sense.

chilled	**sea level**	**wilderness**	**frosty**
forecast	**elevation**	**exposure**	**snowstorm**
directions	**protection**		

Vinson and Annabelle Goodwin did not hear the weather **(1)** _____ on November 13, 1994. So they did not know a **(2)** _____ was coming. They were traveling on an Arizona road at a high **(3)** _____ at the time. In fact, they were more than a mile above **(4)** _____. The Goodwins ran out of gas. But a police officer gave them enough gas to get back to Seligman.

But the Goodwins took a wrong turn. Before long, they got lost in the **(5)** _____ just as the storm arrived. The blowing snow made everything around them look white and **(6)** _____. Then the Goodwins ran out of gas again.

Vinson Goodwin hoped that someone would come along to help. Finally, two hunters drove by and stopped. Vinson Goodwin asked the hunters for **(7)** _____. Then he began walking. But he did not have much **(8)** _____ from the cold. The cold air quickly **(9)** _____ him. He died of **(10)** _____. Annabelle Goodwin was rescued from the van two weeks later.

Cloud Types

There are many different types of clouds. Some clouds bring snow or rain. Some clouds are high in the air. The three main types are **cirrus**, **cumulus**, and **stratus**. The chart below describes these three types of clouds. Study the chart. Circle the answer to each question.

Cirrus		These thin, feather-like clouds are made of tiny bits of ice. They are 20,000 to 45,000 feet high in the sky. Weather is fair.
Cumulus		These clouds are big and puffy. When they are tall and dark, they can bring heavy rain. Their flat bottoms can be as low as 6,000 feet.
Stratus		These clouds look like low, flat sheets. Sometimes they bring rain or snow. The bottoms of the clouds are below 6,000 feet in the sky.

1. Which clouds are the highest in the sky?

cirrus   cumulus   stratus

2. Which clouds look like sheets?

cirrus   cumulus   stratus

3. Which clouds do not bring rain, snow, or hail?

cirrus   cumulus   stratus

4. How do cumulus clouds look?

big and puffy   like feathers   like small clumps

5. Where are the bottoms of stratus clouds?

above 20,000 feet   above 6,000 feet   below 6,000 feet

The Blizzard
of 1996

Light **flurries** began to fall in New York City, New York, on January 7, 1996. These flurries soon turned to heavy snow. At first, the snow built up to just a few inches. That didn't bother New Yorkers. They were used to getting a few inches of snow now and then. But this storm was different. It didn't end with a few inches. Hour after hour, heavy snow kept falling. The storm continued for two straight days. By the time the storm ended, New York City was deep in snow. Parts of the city had more than two feet of new snow.

Too Much Snow

No one in New York was ready for such a huge snowstorm. Mayor Rudolph Giuliani said, "The city is being hit with the largest storm it's ever had." One of the biggest problems the city faced was finding a place to put all the snow. In the country, trucks could just **plow** it off the side of the road. But that wouldn't work in the city. Stores, houses, and office buildings lined the streets. In addition, there were sidewalks and parking meters in the way. So the snow had to be piled into trucks. The trucks then dumped it into the East River. That took days to do. In the meantime, most New York streets remained full of snow.

With the streets blocked, **transportation** became a huge problem. No buses could run. Trains and airplanes stopped running, too. "No trains, no cabs, no nothing — just snow," said one New Yorker.

The snow was so deep and heavy that it even shut down the post office. The U.S. Postal Service takes pride in always being able to deliver the mail in any

Trucks dumped snow into the East River.

kind of weather. But the weather in this storm proved to be too much even for them. "Nothing like this has ever happened before," said Andy Sozzi of the U.S. Postal Service.

Getting to Work

Most New Yorkers gave up trying to get to work. But some people couldn't take the day off. Doctors and nurses still had to care for their many **patients**. Dr. Winston Mitchell wouldn't let the blizzard stop him from doing his job. "I am a **physician**," he said. "It is a job I must go to. People get sick."

On January 8, Mitchell **shoveled** his driveway in hopes of driving to work. But each time he cleared it out, a **snowplow** came down the street. The plow pushed piles of snow back into Mitchell's driveway.

At last, Mitchell gave up shoveling. He set out on foot. He walked through street after street of heavy

Many people skied on the streets in order to get to work.

snow. After three miles of walking, he finally reached his office.

Mitchell wasn't the only one who had trouble getting to work. Dr. Guy Shochat spent an hour and a half trying to dig out his car. It was buried in a snowdrift. At last, he stopped digging. He put on a pair of skis. Shochat skied his way through the streets. He made it to his job at Kings County Hospital. He handles **emergencies** there. He was four hours late, but at least he got there.

Some people found that skiing in this blizzard could be very dangerous. The blowing snow made it hard to see. The high **velocity** winds made it hard to stand up. Vivian Toan tried to ski across the Brooklyn Bridge. "I almost got blown off," she said. "I had to hang on to some of the **cables**."

A Storm to Remember

While most people couldn't get to work, others were trapped at work. Daniel Jackson was an ambulance driver. During the blizzard, he helped out in his company's office. The person who answered the phones couldn't make it in. So Jackson took over.

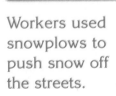

Workers used snowplows to push snow off the streets.

Millions of people in New York will never forget the blizzard of 1996.

For 42 straight hours, he took all the emergency calls. He also radioed his fellow ambulance drivers and told them where they needed to go.

Plenty of people needed ambulances. Some people slipped in the snow and broke bones. A few people even got hit by snowplows. Some people had heart attacks while shoveling snow. In all, at least 100 people died because of the storm.

The blizzard closed schools for two days. It was the first time in 18 years that a snowstorm had shut down the schools. Kyle and Travis Schomburg watched the snow fall outside their New York home. "To the kids, it is all a game," said Aysha Schomburg, their aunt.

Aysha had to stay with Kyle and Travis. The children's mother worked at a hospital. She had to get to work somehow. She waited for a ride that never came. So, like Dr. Mitchell, she ended up walking to work. The children's father, on the other hand, was trapped at his job. He couldn't get home.

"There is no way we have ever had to deal with something like this," said Aysha Schomburg. She was just one of millions of people who would never forget the blizzard of 1996.

Read and Remember — Choose the Answer

❄ **Circle the best ending for each sentence.**

1. Where was the snow dumped?

into the streets   into the East River   around the airport

2. How did Dr. Winston Mitchell get to work?

He flew a plane.   He walked.   He rode a bike.

3. How did Dr. Guy Shochat get to work?

on skis   in a truck   on a train

4. What made it hard to see?

heavy fog   blowing snow   strong rain

5. What happened to the city's schools?

They became hospitals.   They closed.   They opened.

6. How many people died because of the storm?

fewer than five   twenty-five   one hundred

Think About It — Find the Main Idea

❄ **Underline the two most important ideas from the story.**

1. In 1996 Rudolph Giuliani was mayor of New York City.

2. The U.S. Postal Service takes pride in always being able to deliver the mail.

3. A blizzard dumped two feet of snow on New York City.

4. The blizzard made it hard for people to get to work.

5. Daniel Jackson worked for 42 hours straight.

Focus on Vocabulary — Finish Up

Choose the correct word in dark print to complete each sentence.

flurries	**velocity**	**plow**	**emergencies**
cables	**transportation**	**snowplow**	**physician**
shoveled	**patients**		

1. A _____ is another name used for someone who is a doctor.

2. A machine that moves snow out of the way is a _____.

3. Planes, trains, and cars are forms of _____.

4. Speed means _____.

5. Gusts of snow are called _____.

6. To push snow off the road is to _____ it.

7. Things that need immediate care or help are _____.

8. People who are cared for by doctors are _____.

9. Strong, thick ropes or wires are _____.

10. To have scooped snow out of the way is to have _____ it.

Weather Map

A **weather map** shows what kind of weather to expect in an area. The map below shows one day's weather in the United States, Canada, and Mexico. The **map key** explains what the symbols or colors on the map mean. Study the map. Circle the answer to each question.

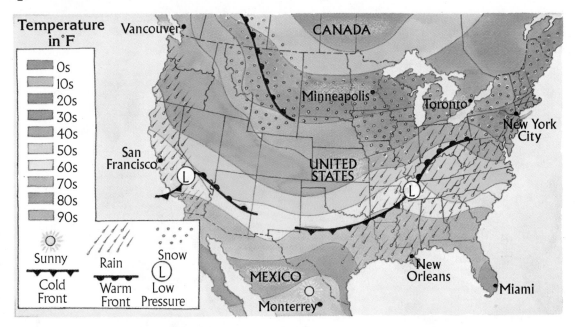

1. Which is the symbol for snow?

2. What color is used to show a temperature of 10°F?

   light blue   dark blue   green

3. What is the weather like in San Francisco?

   sunny   rainy   snowy

4. Which city has about the same temperature as Toronto?

   Minneapolis   Vancouver   Miami

5. Which city could be having a blizzard?

   New Orleans   Monterrey   New York City

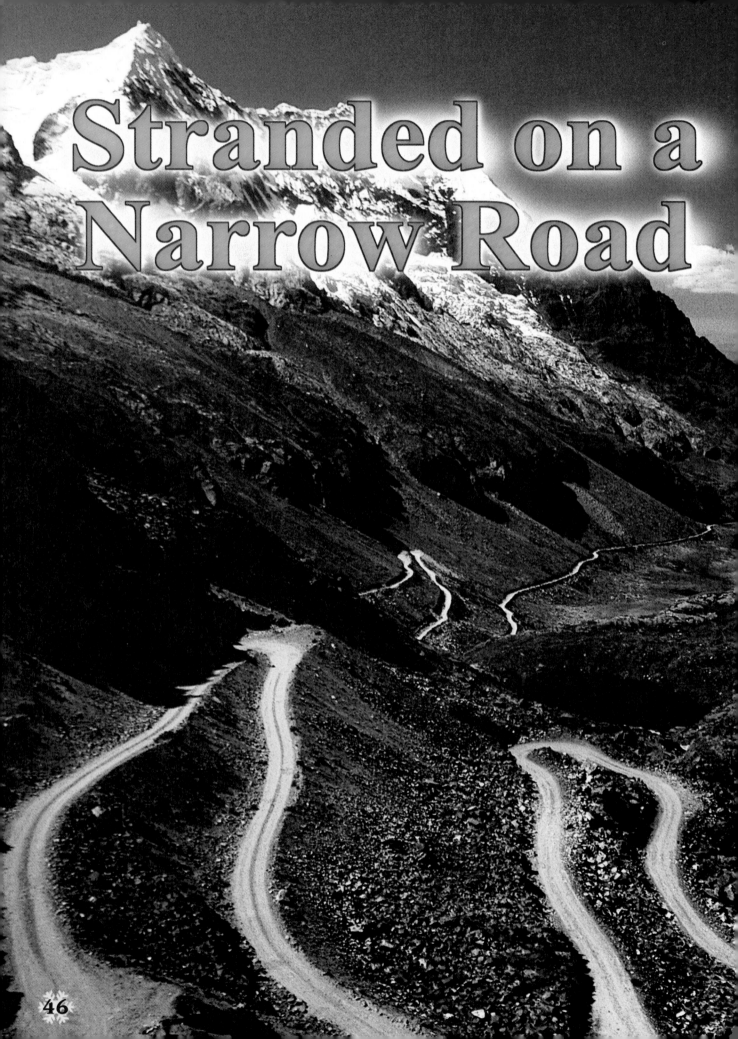

Stranded on a Narrow Road

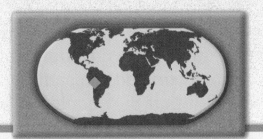

The driver steered the bus along the **narrow** mountain road. He had to be careful. On one side was a high wall of rock. On the other side was a **cliff** that dropped hundreds of feet. If the bus slipped off the road on either side, the driver and all forty passengers could be killed.

The bus driver knew that. But he was used to the danger. Every day he drove through this part of the Andes Mountains in the South American country of Peru. He knew how to handle the narrow, winding roads. But on August 7, 1997, he faced a different danger.

Stuck in the Snow

On that day, a sudden storm swept through Peru. It began late in the day. The storm brought heavy rain to the **capital** city of Lima. Up in the mountains, the air was colder. There, the **precipitation** was snow.

The heaviest snow fell in Negro Mayoc. That was an area about 290 miles from Lima. The elevation of Negro Mayoc was over 11,000 feet. Not many people lived way up there. But a narrow road wound through the area. **Travelers** used it to get from one side of the Andes Mountains to the other.

On this day, thousands of travelers were spread out along the road. Some were in cars. Others were in buses. When the snow began to fall, drivers had no choice. They kept going, hoping to get out of the mountains before the storm got too bad.

Some drivers made it out in time. But others did not. The snow built up quickly. It covered the road like a thick white blanket. With each inch that fell, drivers found it harder and harder to move their cars forward.

One car after another became stuck in the snow. Soon many cars were trapped on the road.

Bus drivers had the same problem. So much snow had fallen that they couldn't plow their way through it. Ten buses became trapped in the snow. That meant that more than 400 passengers on the buses were trapped, too.

Colder and Colder

Meteorologists thought that the storm would be over by the end of the day. But the storm continued to blow all night and all the next day. The **stranded** travelers curled up on their seats, trying to stay warm. The buses had no heat. To make matters even worse, many passengers were not wearing winter clothes. So as the temperature dropped below zero, people became very cold. Most of the passengers had no food, either. So they were hungry as well as cold.

Hour after hour the snow fell. Soon another day had come and gone. Yet the storm still **raged** on. People could no longer see out their car windows. The windows were covered with snow. The bus

Many people travel in buses to cross the mountains of Peru.

The blizzard raged on for days.

windows were higher off the ground but the snow was piled as high as the windows. So some of the bus windows were covered with snow, too.

By this time, everyone on the bus was shivering. Some people began to show signs of **hypothermia**. That meant their body temperature was getting too low. Their hearts were beating slower and slower. They were beginning to freeze to death.

Down in Lima, Peru, **officials** were worried. They wanted to help the travelers trapped in the storm. But there was no way to reach them. The road to Negro Mayoc was completely blocked. Officials kept hoping the storm would end. But day after day the snow just kept falling.

Rescue Work

Finally, on August 11, army leader Homero Nureno sent two helicopters up into the mountains. The two helicopters were loaded with hot food and clothing. The pilots tried their best to get into the Negro Mayoc area. But the storm made it impossible. At times, the pilots couldn't see where they were going. The powerful wind almost blew them into the cliffs. Finally, they turned the helicopters around and headed home. They were lucky to get back to Lima safely.

The next day, rescue workers tried again to reach the travelers. Snowplows and big trucks began trying to push their way up the road into Negro Mayoc. By then, the road was covered with five feet of snow.

"The rescue is difficult because the snow continues falling and the wind is blowing," said rescue worker Hernan Bustamente. "When we clear one stretch of road it snows over again."

Still, the workers kept trying. At last, their heavy plows managed to push through the snow. They reached one bus, then another and another. They chained the buses to their trucks. Then they slowly dragged the buses down out of the mountains. They pulled the stranded cars down, too.

By then, six people had frozen to death. More than one hundred more were very close to dying. This part of the beautiful Andes Mountains had turned into a death trap. Only the brave work of the rescue workers kept it from being even worse.

People had been trapped on the mountain roads for days.

Read and Remember — Check the Events

❄ Place a check in front of the three sentences that tell what happened in the story.

_____ **1.** Heavy snow fell in the Andes Mountains.

_____ **2.** The police closed the roads so no one could leave the area.

_____ **3.** People were stuck on buses with no heat.

_____ **4.** Homero Nureno drove a bus through deep snow.

_____ **5.** No one tried to clear the road for several weeks.

_____ **6.** Six people froze to death.

Write About It

❄ Imagine you had a family member on one of the trapped buses. Write a journal entry describing how you felt as you waited for news of his or her rescue.

_____

_____

_____

_____

_____

_____

_____

_____

_____

_____

Focus on Vocabulary — Make a Word

Choose a word in dark print to complete each sentence. Write the letters of the word on the blanks. When you are finished, the letters in the circles will tell what rescuers first tried to use to reach the people trapped on the road.

travelers   **hypothermia**   **raged**   **cliff**

officials   **meteorologists**   **capital**   **narrow**

stranded   **precipitation**

1. People began to show signs of _____.

     _ _ _ _ _ _〇_ _ _ _

2. The storm _____ on for two days.

     _ _〇_ _ _

3. One side of the mountain was a _____.

     _ _〇_ _ _

4. The _____ in the mountains was snow.

     _ _ _ _ _ _〇_ _ _ _ _ _

5. City _____ sent in rescuers to help the travelers.

     _ _ _ _〇_ _ _ _ _

6. The _____ said the storm would end in a day.

     _ _ _ _ _ _〇_ _ _ _ _ _ _

7. Lima is the _____ city of Peru.

     _ _〇_ _ _ _ _

8. Many people were _____ in the bad weather.

     _ _ _ _〇_ _ _ _

9. There were many _____ on the road.

     _ _ _〇_ _ _ _ _

10. The road in the mountains is very _____.

     _ _〇_ _ _ _

Kinds of Precipitation

Clouds and the **temperature** of the air affect the type of **precipitation** that can form. There are four main types of precipitation. They are rain, snow, **hail**, and **sleet**. Study the information below. Circle the word that best completes each sentence.

Rain

Water droplets join together in clouds. When the drops are heavy enough, they fall as rain.

Snow

If the temperature is freezing, water vapor changes into tiny ice crystals. The ice crystals stick together and form snowflakes.

Hail

Water droplets pass through cold and warm layers of air. They freeze and collect water many times before falling as hail.

Sleet

If raindrops fall through very cold air, they can freeze. The frozen raindrops fall to the ground as sleet.

1. To form rain, water droplets must _____.

    separate   join together   melt

2. If water vapor changes into tiny ice crystals, _____ might fall.

    snow   rain   hail

3. The temperature must be _____ for snow to fall.

    freezing   warm   hot

4. Hail forms when water droplets pass through cold and warm layers of _____.

    snow   air   ice

5. Frozen raindrops are called _____.

    sprinkles   heavy rain   sleet

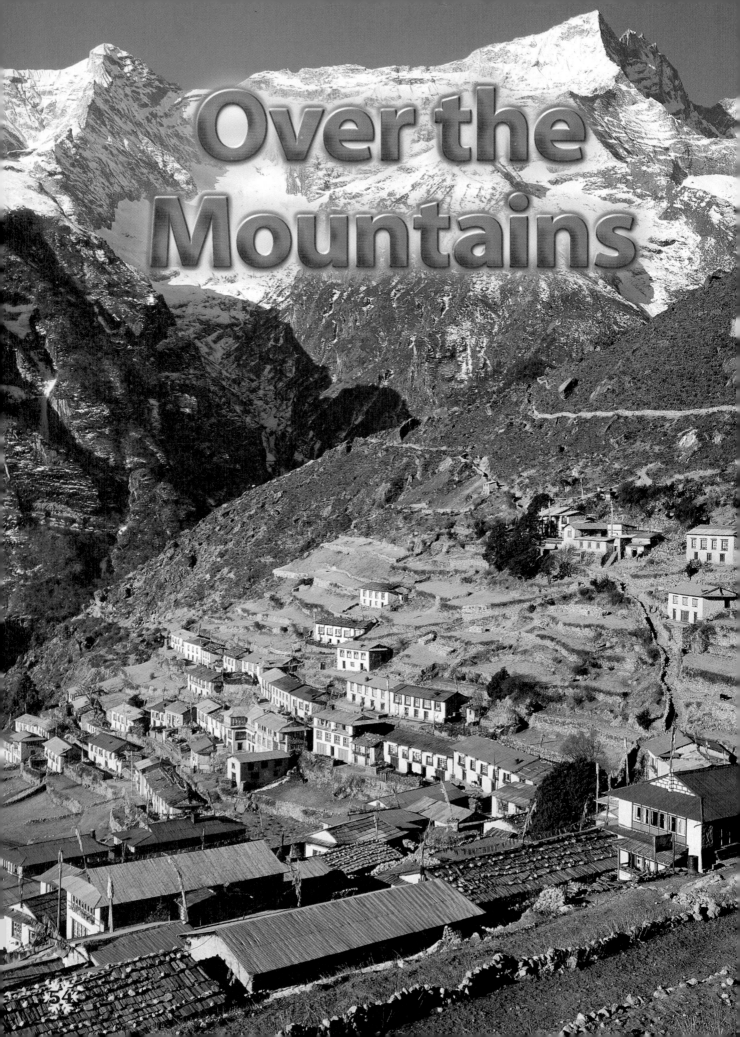

Over the Mountains

Taga knew the **journey** would be very hard. But he felt he had to go. So in December of 1997, he and his girlfriend Chemi left their homes in the Asian land of Tibet. They hoped to make it to the country of Nepal. To get there, they would have to cross the Himalayan Mountains. That meant climbing through the highest mountain **range** in the world. If they were lucky, they would get to Nepal in about 25 days. If they were not so lucky, they would die in the cold and snow of the mountains.

A Dangerous Journey

Taga was sad to leave Tibet. It was the only home he had ever known. But he did not feel free there. Chinese leaders controlled Tibet. These leaders wanted Tibetans to give up their native **customs**. To keep from doing that, Taga and Chemi decided to leave. They headed for the country of Nepal.

They could not travel openly. The Chinese leaders did not want them to go. So they had to sneak out. The only way to do that was over the Himalayas. They joined a group of 19 other Tibetans. Traveling on foot, they all headed west across the mountains.

This group was not the first one to leave Tibet. Thousands of other Tibetans had made the same dangerous journey. In 1993 a woman named Yandol and two friends did it. They wanted very much to be free. They packed some food. Each one took a coat and a blanket. Then they began the long, hard climb.

After a few days, they were 18,000 feet above sea level. That meant they were much higher than North

The Himalayas are the world's highest mountain range.

America's Rocky Mountains. At such a high **altitude**, the snow never melted. Rocks and cliffs were covered with ice. If the women took one wrong step, they could fall hundreds of feet to their death.

At night, they curled up in the snow and tried to sleep. The wind blew hard all around them. They wrapped themselves tightly in their blankets and hoped they wouldn't freeze to death.

The daytime was not much better. "For two days we had to walk inside a stream," Yandol said. "The **canyon** walls were too **steep**. There was no other way but to go in the water." She was wearing thin **canvas** shoes. The icy water quickly soaked through them. "At first it hurt like a thousand needles," Yandol said. "But after a while my feet just went numb."

At last she and her friends made it to Nepal. By then, they were half frozen and they could barely walk. But they were alive.

Ice and Snow All Around

In 1995 a Tibetan man named Kersan made it over the mountains with his 6-year-old daughter. They, too, faced wind, ice, and cold. One of Kersan's toes turned black from frostbite. But he couldn't let that stop him. He kept walking. Kersan kept going for himself and his daughter.

Day after day, Kersan and his daughter dragged themselves along. They were cold and hungry but most of all, they were thirsty. They nearly died from thirst. They didn't see the stream that Yandol walked through. They found no water at all. There was ice and snow all around them, but that wasn't much help. They couldn't eat enough snow to give them the water they needed. Trying to do so would have made them even colder. Then their body temperature would have lowered too much.

Dr. David R. Shlim knew what Kersan and others went through. Shlim worked in Nepal. He cared for many of the people who made it over the mountains. "What the Tibetans **endure** is almost unbelievable," Shlim said. "They cross the highest mountains in the world. They have no tents, no sleeping bags, and they are often wearing only **windbreakers** and sneakers."

Bad Weather

When Taga and Chemi set out, they were hoping for good weather. But after eight days, they ran into

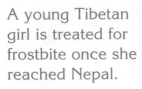

A young Tibetan girl is treated for frostbite once she reached Nepal.

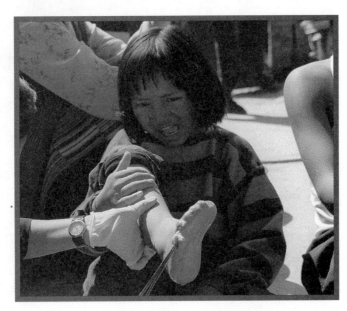

a blizzard. They were at 18,000 feet when it struck. Icy snow and wind cut into their faces. The falling snow made it harder and harder to walk. Taga saw 11-year-old Shilok Dolma fall down. She didn't have the strength to go on. Taga picked her up. All day he carried her on his back. But by night she was dead.

Soon after that, Taga himself fell down. Chemi picked him up. For two days, she carried him on her back. His feet hurt terribly from frostbite. Sometimes Chemi stopped and put them against her bare skin to warm them. Still, the frostbite crept deeper and deeper into Taga's body.

For three days and nights, the snow kept falling. At last it stopped. The group **staggered** into Nepal. There, Taga had to have his feet removed. The frostbite had turned them black. Still, he was one of the lucky ones. Five members of the group had died in the blizzard.

Taga had made it to Nepal but frostbite had ruined his feet.

USE WHAT YOU KNOW

Read and Remember — Choose the Answer

❄ **Draw a circle around the correct answer.**

1. What mountains did Taga cross?

Andes   Himalayas   Rockies

2. Who did not want the Tibetans to leave?

Chinese leaders   Nepalese leaders   Indian leaders

3. What did Yandol and her friends take with them?

plenty of money   a blanket and coat   guns and knives

4. Where did Yandol sleep at night?

in the snow   in small holes   in trees

5. Who carried Taga for two days?

his girlfriend   a Chinese leader   a young boy

Think About It — Cause and Effect

❄ A **cause** is something that makes something else happen. What happens is called the **effect**. Match each cause with an effect. Write the letter on the correct blank. The first one is done for you.

Cause	Effect
1. Taga couldn't walk, so ___c___	**a.** he and his daughter almost died from thirst.
2. Kersan could not find water, so _____	**b.** they made the dangerous journey to Nepal.
3. Chemi wanted to warm Taga's toes, so _____	**c.** Chemi carried him.
4. Taga and Chemi wanted to keep their customs, so _____	**d.** she put them on her bare skin.

59

Focus on Vocabulary — Finish the Paragraphs

Use the words in dark print to complete the paragraphs.
Reread the paragraphs to be sure they make sense.

endure	**altitude**	**customs**	**range**	**windbreakers**
canvas	**journey**	**steep**	**canyon**	**staggered**

In 1997 Taga and his girlfriend Chemi left Tibet and set out on
a dangerous **(1)** _____. They crossed the highest mountain
(2) _____ in the world. It is very cold and stormy there.
A blizzard hit them when they were at an **(3)** _____ of
18,000 feet. By the time they **(4)** _____ out of the
mountains, they were barely alive.

Many other Tibetans made the same trip. They wanted to be
free to practice their native **(5)** _____. They were willing
to **(6)** _____ great pain to get to a place where they could
do that. Many of them faced the cold, bitter blizzards wearing just
(7) _____. A woman named Yandol walked through an
icy stream at the bottom of a **(8)** _____. On her feet, she
wore thin **(9)** _____ shoes. The icy water soaked through
them. But Yandol had no choice. The tall, rocky walls were too
(10) _____ for her to climb. Like Taga and Chemi, she
barely made it to Nepal alive.

Mountain Heights

The Himalayas are a tall mountain **range** in Asia. Mount Everest is part of the Himalayas. It is the highest mountain on Earth. The diagram below shows the highest mountains of six continents. Study the diagram. Circle the answer to each question.

| Mt. Kosciusko 7,310 ft. Australia | Mt. Elbrus 18,510 ft. Europe | Kilimanjaro 19,340 ft. Africa | Mt. McKinley 20,320 ft. South America | Aconcagua 22,831 ft. South America | Mt. Everest 29,028 ft. Asia |

1. What is the height of Mount Everest?

   29,028 feet   18,510 feet   19,340 feet

2. Which mountain has a height of 22,831 feet?

   Mount Elbrus   Aconcagua   Kilimanjaro

3. Where is Kilimanjaro?

   Europe   South America   Africa

4. Which is the highest of these three mountains?

   Kilimanjaro   Mount Elbrus   Mount McKinley

5. Which continent has the lowest of the six mountains?

   Asia   Australia   Europe

Twelve Long Days

George Back wanted to go on a **snowmobile** ride. His wife, Diane McManus, did, too. Back and McManus were on a trip in Washington's Cascade Mountains. They had never been on snowmobiles before. It sounded like a nice way to spend the day. On January 27, 1999, they rented two snowmobiles. They planned to take a two-hour ride through the mountains near Fish Lake. They did not know that this short ride would forever change their lives.

Lost

Back and McManus dressed warmly for the ride. They each put on a **snowsuit** and new boots. They did not plan to be gone very long. So they didn't pack any food. But they did bring their dogs. Back and McManus had two little Yorkshire **terriers** named Keeper and Justine. They loved these dogs very much. They didn't want to leave them alone. So McManus tucked one dog inside her snowsuit. Back tucked the other inside his snowsuit. Then they climbed onto the rented snowmobiles and rode off into the snowy mountains.

The couple planned to stay on the trail. But somehow they took a wrong turn. They got lost. Soon they found themselves in deep snow. When the snowmobiles got stuck, neither Back nor McManus could get them out.

Looking around, Back wasn't sure what to do. He didn't know where he was. He didn't know how to get back to the hotel. Besides, he was not in good shape. There was no way he could have walked very far through the deep snow.

At last, he and McManus decided to stay where they were. They hoped someone would come along to help them. As the hours passed, they got tired. They lay down in the snow. Keeper and Justine curled up next to them and helped keep them warm.

A Search Finds Nothing

When night came, people back at the hotel became worried. Back and McManus had not returned yet. Officials sent people out to look for them. Rescuers rode snowmobiles over miles of snowy trails. Rescue planes flew low over the mountains. But no one found any sign of the missing couple. At last, after four days of searching, the rescuers gave up. They thought that Back and McManus had probably died somewhere out in the cold wilderness.

In fact, Back was still alive. He was cold and hungry and growing weaker. But he was not dead.

Rescuers work to get George Back out of the snow.

For twelve days he lay in the snow. His dogs stayed right next to him. Diane McManus lay nearby. At some point, McManus died. Somehow, though, Back hung on to life.

During this time, a snowstorm hit. It dropped four feet of snow on the area. Back did not have the strength to move. So he just let the snow cover him.

He didn't know it at the time, but the snow helped save his life. When snow is loosely packed, it is very good **insulation**. That means it helps keep out the cold. Air gets trapped between each **snowflake**. Body heat warms that trapped air. That's what happened to George Back. His body heat warmed the air trapped in the snow around him.

Surprisingly, the fact that Back was overweight also helped him. The extra weight on his body acted as insulation. It kept him from losing too much body heat. Finally, Keeper and Justine helped. The dogs stayed with Back the whole time. That gave him a little extra warmth.

Still, no one can last forever in the snow. By February 7, Back's body temperature was down to about 95 degrees **Fahrenheit**. He had frostbite on his feet, knees, elbows, and nose. He was getting closer and closer to death.

A Boot in the Snow

Luckily, a man named Darrell Brunner went out on his snowmobile that day. Brunner and three friends decided to take a ride up near Brushy Creek. That was a **remote** area up in the mountains. It was 10 miles from Fish Lake. "We went to that area just on a **whim**," Brunner said.

As Brunner and his friends rode through the heavy snow, they heard dogs barking. Looking around, they saw two terriers lying next to a black boot. Brunner stopped and began brushing snow off the boot. He found George Back lying face down. Back was buried in almost five feet of snow. But he was alive. "Those little **teeny** dogs were no bigger than rats," Brunner said. "But I think they helped save his life."

It was hard to believe that George Back had made it through twelve days in the snow. He had lost a lot of weight. He had a terrible case of frostbite. He was also very upset over the death of his wife. But as one newspaper said, it was **stunning** that George Back was alive at all.

Back was rushed to a hospital after his rescue.

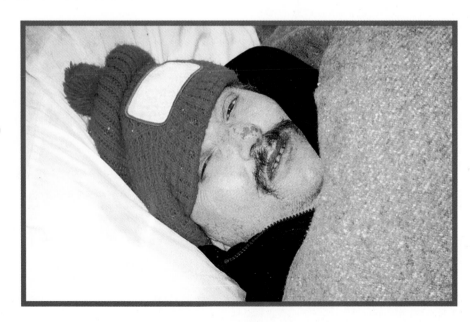

Read and Remember — Finish the Sentence

❄ Circle the best ending for each sentence.

1. Back and McManus loved their two little _____.

birds   dogs   daughters

2. Back and McManus did not make it back to the _____.

hotel   train station   airport

3. For twelve days, Back lay in the _____.

water   snow   dirt

4. Back's body temperature _____.

rose   dropped   stayed the same

5. Darrell Brunner and his friends heard _____.

crying   an engine running   dogs barking

Write About It

❄ Imagine that you are Darrell Brunner. Write a letter to a friend, describing how you felt when you found George Back.

Dear _____,

_____

_____

_____

_____

_____

_____

Focus on Vocabulary — Crossword Puzzle

Use the clues to complete the puzzle. Choose from the words in dark print.

insulation	**terriers**	**snowflake**	**Fahrenheit**	**whim**
snowmobile	**remote**	**snowsuit**	**stunning**	**teeny**

Across

3. very small

4. a sudden idea

5. material that keeps in heat

7. surprising

9. machine that moves on snow

Down

1. suit worn in cold snow

2. a scale for measuring heat

3. small dogs

6. a small crystal of snow

8. far away from a city

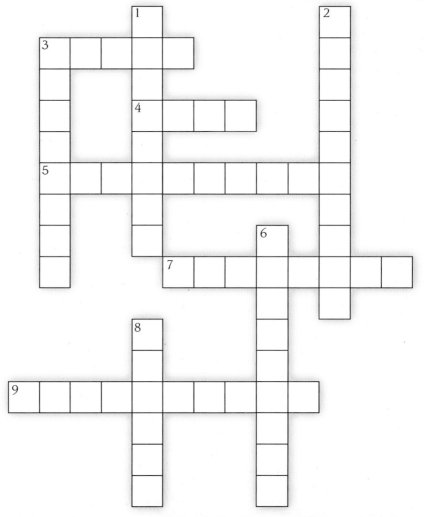

Thermometers

People use thermometers to measure **temperature**. Temperature is measured in **degrees**. One thermometer below measures temperature in degrees **Fahrenheit**, or °F. The other thermometer uses degrees **Celsius**, or °C. Circle the answer that best completes each sentence.

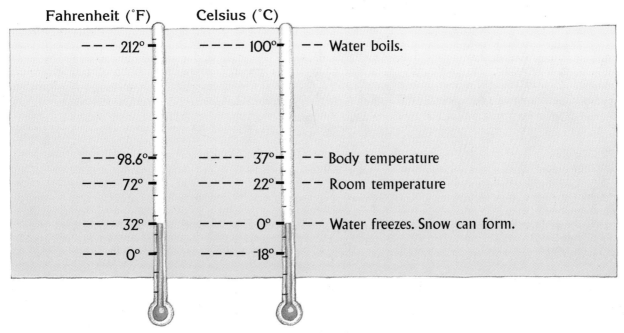

Fahrenheit (°F)   Celsius (°C)

— 212° — 100° — Water boils.

— 98.6° — 37° — Body temperature
— 72° — 22° — Room temperature

— 32° — 0° — Water freezes. Snow can form.
— 0° — -18°

1. Water freezes at 32°F and at _____.

32°C   100°C   0°C

2. 98.6°F is the normal temperature of _____.

a person's body   many rooms   boiling water

3. The _____ thermometer shows that water boils at 100°.

Fahrenheit   Celsius   bigger

4. Snow is most likely to form when the air is _____.

102°F   32°F   55°C

5. 21°C is warmer than _____.

37°C   32°F   80°F

Buried Under the Snow

It snows a lot in the Austrian Alps. Every year these European mountains get up to 20 feet of snow. That's why the Alps are such a great place for people who love to ski. People come from around the world to ski in these mountains. But in February of 1999, the Alps got more snow than people had ever seen. Day after day the snow fell. On some days, as much as six feet came down. Snow was piling up everywhere. Soon everyone was hoping the snow would stop.

A Killer Avalanche

The heavy snow caused roads to be closed. Food had to be flown in. Even then, some people couldn't get out of their homes or hotels. After a while, no one knew how much snow had fallen. All of the tools used to measure **snowfall** had been buried.

Along with the snow came terrible winds. In some places the wind whipped at more than 175 miles an hour. That made it as strong as a **hurricane**.

People knew that the snow and wind could cause avalanches. Avalanches often struck in the Alps. Most of the time, however, they didn't do much harm. This is because heavy steel fences had been put up on many mountains. These fences stopped whatever snow came sliding down.

But this year, the fences were not enough. There was just too much snow in Austria. Huge waves of snow plowed right over the fences.

The avalanche that struck the ski village of Galtur, Austria, was among the worst. The avalanche hit just

Heavy snowfall buried many towns in the Alps in 1999.

after 4:00 P.M. on February 23. A wall of snow 16 feet high roared down the mountain. It cut the top off one house "like a **razor** blade." Many other homes were completely buried. The snow and ice tossed cars around like toys.

Most people in the village of Galtur never saw the avalanche coming. "Suddenly, it started," said Franz Wenko, a hotel owner. "The lights went out. It was dark. There was only dust and snow."

"I thought it was just a storm," said 17-year-old Hanno Heinz. Then snow blew open the locked windows in the hotel where he was staying.

Some people were buried under piles of snow 30 feet high. That was higher than a two-story house. Those people who escaped began digging to save their friends and family members. All they had to work with was a few shovels and their bare hands. Rescuers from other towns couldn't reach Galtur until morning because the weather was so bad. Snow blocked the roads. People in the village did manage to save 20 lives. But more than 30 others died. It was one of the worst **natural disasters** ever to hit Austria.

Survivors were filled with sadness and **disbelief**. "No one expected this," said one official. Everyone had thought Galtur was a safe village. After all, no avalanche had struck there in more than 300 years. But in the winter of 1999, no place was safe.

Alexander

February 24 brought still more bad news. A second avalanche hit the nearby village of Valzur. A huge wall of snow buried many people there. Rescuers used long poles to poke down through piles of snow, looking for survivors. They also brought in trained dogs to help with the search. After two hours, they were losing hope of finding anyone alive. Then one of the dogs found Alexander.

Alexander was a four-year-old boy who had been buried by the avalanche. When he was first pulled from the snow, it looked as though he was dead. He was not breathing. Rescuers couldn't find a **pulse**. Still, they thought there was a chance of saving him. They blew air into his **lungs**. It worked. Slowly, Alexander began to show signs of life.

Rescuers search the snow for survivors of the avalanche.

One Happy Ending

No one could believe that the little boy had lived through the avalanche. People began to call him "the **miracle** of Valzur." Doctors said it was his small size that saved him. A grown person buried so long would have died. In fact, most people would have **survived** no more than 15 minutes.

Most people would have died from lack of **oxygen**. But Alexander didn't run out of oxygen. His body was so small that it cooled down very quickly. As his body got colder, his heart slowed down. His whole body used less and less oxygen. So he was able to stay alive with what little air he had.

Rescuers wrapped Alexander in blankets. They slowly warmed up his body. Then they flew him to the hospital. The next day he was back to normal. "The boy is well," said his doctor. "He eats normally. He talks and plays." Alexander's story was one bright spot in a week of sadness.

An avalanche struck the village of Valzur on February 24.

Read and Remember — Check the Events

🌨 Place a check in front of the three sentences that tell what happened in the story.

_____ **1.** Avalanches hit the Austrian villages of Galtur and Valzur.

_____ **2.** People were buried under piles of snow 30 feet high.

_____ **3.** A four-year-old boy named Alexander was found alive.

_____ **4.** In Valzur, Austria, a doctor fell through the ice.

_____ **5.** Wind blew the roof off one hotel.

_____ **6.** Police would not let anyone ski in the Austrian Alps.

Think About It — Find the Main Ideas

🌨 Underline the two most important ideas from the story.

1. Franz Wenko owned a hotel in Galtur, Austria.

2. In February 1999, huge amounts of snow fell in the Austrian Alps.

3. Snow blew open Hanno Heinz's locked windows.

4. Avalanches buried people, houses, and roads.

5. Rescuers wrapped Alexander in blankets.

Focus on Vocabulary — Find the Meaning

Read each sentence. Circle the best meaning for the word or words in dark print.

1. The tools used to measure **snowfall** had been buried.

   weight of snow   the amount of snow   time of snow

2. The wind was as strong as a **hurricane**.

   storm with strong winds   flood   metal building

3. It cut off the roof like a **razor** blade.

   handle of a shovel   long   shaving tool

4. It was one of the worst **natural disasters** ever.

   seasons   terrible events in nature   wrecks

5. People were filled with **disbelief**.

   sadness   not much energy   not believing

6. Rescuers couldn't find a **pulse**.

   regular beating in blood vessels   tool   warm place

7. Rescuers blew air into his **lungs**.

   gloves   parts of the body used for breathing   pockets

8. People called him the "**miracle** of Valzur."

   something amazing   last in line   lucky child

9. Most people would not have **survived**.

   been outside   acted quickly   lived

10. Alexander didn't run out of **oxygen**.

    gas in air   hope   places to hide

Snowfall Amounts

❄ Snow usually falls more during certain months of the year than during others. The winter months usually have the greatest **snowfall**. The line graph below shows the snowfall in North America each month in 1998. Study the line graph. Circle the answer to each question.

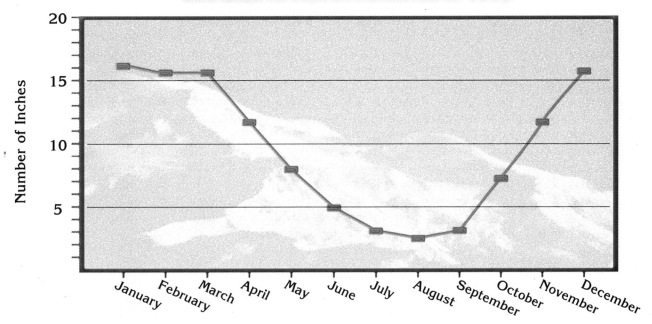

Snowfall in North America in 1998

1. During which month did about 8 inches of snow fall?

March   May   September

2. About how many inches fell in North America in June?

3   5   15

3. In which month did the most snow fall?

January   May   December

4. In which month did the least snow fall?

February   April   August

5. During what time of year does most snow fall?

summer   fall   winter

77

Ice from the Sky

No one thought the weather was going to be bad. On April 14, 1999, the sky over Sydney, Australia, looked clear. At 5:00 that evening, TV **weatherman** Tim Bailey said that it would be sunny and clear for the next several days. Other weathermen **predicted** the same kind of weather. But the weathermen also were wrong. Three hours later, an ice storm hit Sydney. It was one of the worst storms the city had ever seen.

Surprise!

Weatherman Evan Bathe was among the first to see the storm coming. At 6:45 P.M., Bathe picked up signs of rain and clouds on his computer. At that point, the storm was near the south coast of Australia. It looked as if it was headed out to sea. In any case, the storm seemed to be dying. But 15 minutes later, Bathe checked his computer again. He shook his head in disbelief. A second storm had suddenly **developed**. It was big, and it was headed straight for Sydney.

The nightly news was already over. So Bathe had no way to warn the people of Sydney. He did call the airport, though. At 7:15 P.M. he told airport officials that a huge storm was on the way. He said it would strike in less than half an hour.

One plane at the airport was waiting to take off. It had been waiting a long time already. The people on board were in a hurry to get going. But when the captain heard about the storm, he told them that they would have to wait even longer.

This news upset the passengers. But then they saw the storm coming. They could see its dark clouds through the windows of the plane. They felt the storm's high winds begin to rock the plane back and forth. Suddenly, everyone on board grew quiet. They were happy to be on the ground instead of in the air.

Large Chunks of Ice

As the passengers sat in their seats, they heard loud banging sounds. Large chunks of ice were hitting the plane. These chunks are called **hailstones**. "It was like someone was tossing melons at us," said one passenger.

Indeed, the storm that hit Sydney did not bring rain. It was a **hailstorm**. So instead of rain, big pieces of ice fell.

Hailstorms begin when **raindrops** get caught in wind high in the sky. The wind tosses these raindrops up to where the air is very cold. The raindrops freeze into tiny balls of ice. Again and again these balls are tossed up into the very cold air. Each time, the balls

Many hailstones that fell in Sydney were as big as baseballs.

The falling hail smashed cars, buildings, and traffic lights.

of ice gather more and more **moisture**. That makes them get bigger. Finally, the balls of ice fall to the earth as hailstones.

Most hailstones are no bigger than peas. But in this storm, the wind was very strong. It kept tossing the balls of ice around until they were the size of baseballs.

The falling hailstones pounded the outside of the plane. It did great damage. By the time the storm was over, the plane could no longer fly.

Falling ice caused terrible damage all over the city. It broke windows and traffic lights. It knocked down power lines. Hailstones smashed cars. They blasted pieces of roofing off the tops of houses. Margaret Cook counted 17 holes in the roof of her home. "There are holes as big as watermelons in our roof," she said.

Close Calls

The storm almost killed a woman named Robyn Attuel. Attuel was in her home at the time. She

thought she was safe. But as she went upstairs, a hailstone crashed through a **skylight** above her. The hailstone hit her on the head. It cracked her skull. Also, pieces of flying glass cut her. She was very lucky she survived.

Noel Masters was in his bedroom when the storm hit. "It was awful," he said. "I didn't want to get too close to the window. I went into another room." It was a good thing he did. Two large hailstones broke the window and landed on his bed. If he had stayed in his room, he might have been badly **injured**.

Most people ran for cover as the hailstones fell. But the animals outside couldn't do that. In one park, 45 birds tried to fly away to safety. Not one of them made it. "They were just **pelted** out of the sky," said Naomi Welch, a rescue official.

The storm only lasted a few minutes. But its large hailstones were very powerful. It did more damage than any other storm in the history of Australia. The total amount of damage was almost 1 billion dollars. As it turned out, April 14, 1999, wasn't so clear after all.

Read and Remember — Choose the Answer

Draw a circle around the correct answer.

1. What kind of weather did people expect on April 14, 1999?
   cold and wet   clear   very hot

2. What did Evan Bathe do when he realized a storm was coming?
   He ran home.   He called the airport.   He shut doors.

3. What hit the plane that was waiting to take off?
   large chunks of ice   birds   lights

4. Where was Robyn Attuel when she was hit by a hailstone?
   on a mountain   on a beach   in her home

5. How long did the hailstorm last?
   a few minutes   six hours   two days

Write About It

Imagine you were living in Sydney, Australia, on April 14, 1999. Write a letter to a friend, describing the storm.

Dear _____ ,

_____

_____

_____

_____

_____

_____

_____

Focus on Vocabulary — Match Up

Match each word with its meaning. Darken the circle beside the correct answer.

1. weatherman
   ○ person reporting the weather   ○ official   ○ pilot

2. predicted
   ○ forgot   ○ kept from harm   ○ told ahead of time

3. developed
   ○ covered completely   ○ formed   ○ lost weight

4. hailstones
   ○ chunks of ice   ○ small holes   ○ hard bits of rock

5. hailstorm
   ○ disease   ○ storm with hail   ○ loud greeting

6. raindrops
   ○ buckets of water   ○ heavy clouds   ○ drops of rain

7. moisture
   ○ flying glass   ○ wetness   ○ stairs leading up

8. skylight
   ○ weak light   ○ early morning sky   ○ window in a roof

9. injured
   ○ brought inside   ○ hurt   ○ turned around

10. pelted
    ○ hit hard   ○ touched   ○ moved

How Hail Forms

During a storm, a **raindrop** can be blown high in a cloud. Then it freezes in the colder air and becomes ice. As the ice drops, it collects more water. If the ice is blown high again, the water freezes on it. This makes a **hailstone**. The hailstone gets larger and heavier until it falls from the sky. Study the diagram. Write the answer to each question.

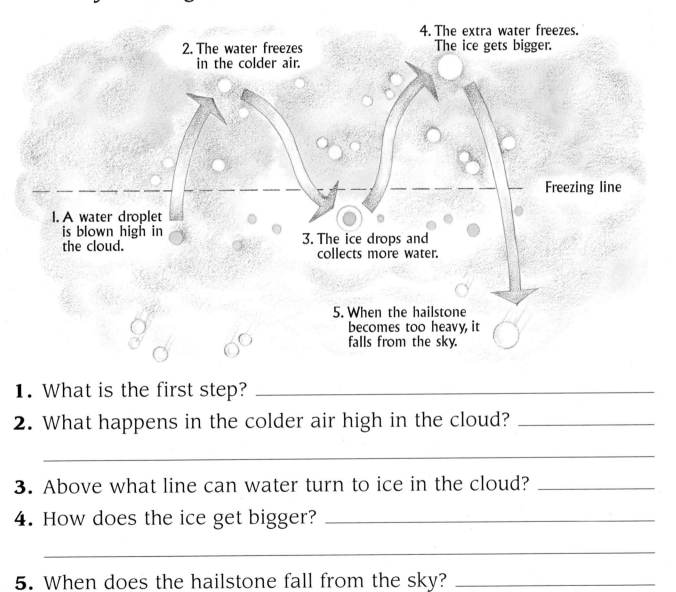

2. The water freezes in the colder air.

4. The extra water freezes. The ice gets bigger.

Freezing line

1. A water droplet is blown high in the cloud.

3. The ice drops and collects more water.

5. When the hailstone becomes too heavy, it falls from the sky.

1. What is the first step? _____

2. What happens in the colder air high in the cloud? _____

_____

3. Above what line can water turn to ice in the cloud? _____

4. How does the ice get bigger? _____

_____

5. When does the hailstone fall from the sky? _____

Race Against Time

r. Jerri Neilsen was in trouble. Neilsen had come to Antarctica in November 1998. That's when she took over as doctor at the Amundsen-Scott South Pole Station. Her job was to care for the 41 people living there. Neilsen planned to stay at the South Pole for one year. The first seven months went well. But in June 1999, Neilsen herself needed help. She discovered a lump in her body that had not been there before. It turned out that Dr. Neilsen had **cancer**.

Trouble at the South Pole

When most people get cancer, they begin to treat it right away. But Neilsen could not do that. She could not go to a hospital where doctors could remove the lump. She did not have any of the medicine she needed. Even worse, there was no easy way for her to get it.

The South Pole is a very **isolated** spot. It is far away from the rest of the world. The **climate** there is terrible. Snow and ice are everywhere. Snowstorms and **windstorms** often last for days. The temperature can be as low as 80 degrees below zero. Finally, there is the darkness. For six months every year, there is no sunshine at all. As one **expert** said, "The South Pole is the highest, driest, emptiest, coldest, darkest, most isolated place on Earth." Because of all this, few people ever go there.

The 41 people who were at the South Pole Station were doing science **research**. They had come in November and December. Those were the only times the weather was good enough for planes to land.

When Neilsen realized she had cancer, she knew she was in trouble. It would be five months before she could get out of Antarctica. She could use her radio to talk to people in other parts of the world. She could use her computer, too. But Neilsen needed more than talk. She needed medicine, and she needed it fast.

A Dangerous Plan

Officials back in the United States wanted to help. On July 12, they sent a special plane to the South Pole. It carried 19 crew members. It also carried the medicine that Neilsen needed.

The plane could not land at the South Pole. If the pilot tried to land the plane there, the engines would freeze. So the crew just planned to fly over the South Pole. They hoped to drop six boxes of medicine down to Dr. Neilsen.

It was a **risky** plan. For one thing, the crew was flying in complete darkness. They might miss the drop-off point. They could also run out of **fuel**.

They might get frostbite during the long trip. When they opened the door to drop the boxes, they could get hypothermia. That would mean their body temperature was getting too low.

It took the plane eight hours to reach the South Pole. By then, the inside of the plane was so cold that a can of soda froze and **exploded**. The crew knew they had to hurry. They were running low on fuel. At last they saw small fires in the snow below them. Workers at the South Pole Station had started these. The fires showed where the boxes should be dropped.

Twice the plane flew low over that spot. Each time, crew members opened the door. In came a rush of incredibly cold air. The crew hurried to drop the boxes of medicine. Then the plane took off for home. By then, the crew was very cold and tired. But they were happy. They had done their job well.

Meanwhile, workers at the South Pole Station had just seven minutes to get the boxes. If they took longer than that, the medicine would freeze. Then it would be no good. Luckily, the workers moved quickly. They got the boxes in time.

Workers had just seven minutes to get the boxes inside the station.

Home at Last

Everyone was happy that the plan had worked so well. But they knew that Neilsen was still in danger. The medicine would keep her cancer from spreading. But she still needed an **operation** to remove it. If she waited too long, the cancer could kill her.

Again, officials in the United States formed a plan. They didn't want to wait until November or December to get Neilsen. So they got a plane ready in October. They chose a man named George McAllister to be the pilot.

On October 23, the temperature at the South Pole rose a little. That day it was only 60 degrees below zero. McAllister thought he could get his plane in and out of the South Pole at that temperature. So he and his crew took off.

When they reached the South Pole, they hurried to get Neilsen on board. Then they managed to get the plane's engines going again. They flew Neilsen home safely. A few days later, she had the operation she needed. It had not been easy. But at last Jerri Neilsen's long wait was over.

The crew was proud they had been able to fly Dr. Neilsen home safely.

Read and Remember — Finish the Sentence

❄ **Circle the best ending for each sentence.**

1. Neilsen found a lump in her body when she was in _____.
   Nebraska   New Zealand   Antarctica

2. Officials wanted to give Neilsen boxes of _____.
   food   medicine   computers

3. For six months every year, the South Pole has no _____.
   wind   sunshine   storms

4. A plane could not land at the South Pole in July, because its engines would _____.
   get too hot   freeze   melt

5. Dr. Jerri Neilsen was finally _____.
   forgotten   flown home   driven away

Think About It — Find the Sequence

❄ **Number the sentences to show the correct order from the story. The first one is done for you.**

_____ **1.** Dr. Jerri Neilsen found a lump in her body.

__1__ **2.** Neilsen took over as doctor at the Amundsen-Scott South Pole Station.

_____ **3.** Neilsen had an operation.

_____ **4.** Workers lit fires to show the plane where to drop the boxes.

_____ **5.** George McAllister took off for the South Pole.

Focus on Vocabulary — Make a Word

Choose a word in dark print to complete each sentence. Write the letters of the word on the blanks. When you are finished, the letters in the circles will tell you who flew the plane that rescued Dr. Jerri Neilsen.

isolated   cancer   research   windstorms   operation

exploded   risky   fuel   climate   expert

1. The South Pole's _____ is cold and windy.

   ◯ _ _ _ _ _ _

2. The lump meant that Dr. Neilsen had _____.

   ◯ _ _ _ _ _ _

3. Workers at the South Pole did _____.

   _ ◯ _ _ _ _ _ _

4. The plane could run out of _____.

   ◯ _ _ _

5. The South Pole is an _____ spot.

   ◯ _ _ _ _ _ _ _

6. Officials came up with a _____ plan.

   ◯ _ _ _ _

7. Cold _____ blew for days in Antarctica.

   ◯ _ _ _ _ _ _ _ _ _

8. One _____ said it was the darkest place on Earth.

   _ _ _ _ _ ◯ _

9. A can of soda _____ on the plane.

   ◯ _ _ _ _ _ _ _

10. Dr. Neilsen needed an _____.

   ◯ _ _ _ _ _ _ _ _

92

Climate Areas

There are three main **climate** areas on Earth. The warmest areas of Earth are near the **equator**. The equator is an imaginary line around the middle of the earth. The **polar** areas are the coldest, because they are farthest from the equator. Study the map below. Write the answer to each question.

Climate Areas

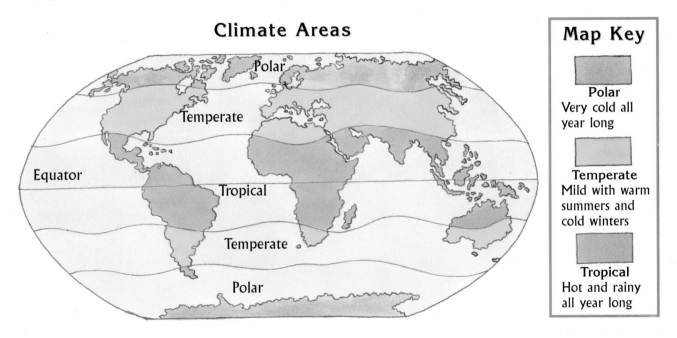

Map Key

Polar Very cold all year long

Temperate Mild with warm summers and cold winters

Tropical Hot and rainy all year long

1. What are the three main climate areas of Earth? _____

_____

2. Which climate area is closest to the equator? _____

3. Which climate area is cold most of the year? _____

4. What is the climate in a temperate area? _____

_____

5. Is a tropical area likely to be warm or cold? _____

Alone in the Snow

On December 24, 1999, Matt Sanders decided to take a short **hike**. Sanders was on vacation in the European country of Switzerland. He was in mountains called the Alps. Sanders wanted to climb a trail near a ski area there. He planned to ride back down on a ski lift before it got dark.

Sanders knew a lot about hiking. So he packed extra clothes and a warm coat. He took plenty of food and water. He even took a sleeping bag in case of an emergency. But Sanders forgot how slow hiking through deep snow can be.

A Sudden Blizzard

The 23-year-old Sanders set out early in the morning. He knew that sudden snowstorms were always possible in this cold climate. But he was only going to be gone a few hours. He thought he would be back long before any bad weather moved in.

Deep snow covered the trail. This snow slowed him down. He couldn't hike as far or as fast as he had hoped. By late afternoon, he was still on the mountain. It began to snow hard. The snowstorm quickly turned into a blizzard. It brought heavy snow and high winds.

Sanders couldn't make it back down the trail. He couldn't get over to the ski lift, either. The blowing snow made it hard to see. Besides, night was coming. It was getting dark. Sanders managed to stay **calm**. He decided the best thing to do would be to spend the night on the mountain.

Looking around, he spotted a tiny cave in the **mountainside**. He crawled into it. Next, he ate some of the food he had brought along. Then Sanders slipped into his sleeping bag. He tried to sleep. Most of all, he tried to stay warm.

The storm grew worse and worse. Officials later called it one of the worst blizzards in history. Winds blew more than 120 miles an hour. The temperatures fell to 22 degrees below zero.

For 48 hours, the storm raged on. Sanders spent all that time in his sleeping bag. He stayed in the bag to help **preserve** his body heat.

After two full days, the snow finally stopped. But the winds kept blowing hard. Sanders left the cave and tried to look around. But the wind was too strong. It slammed him to the ground. He had to crawl on his hands and knees back to the cave.

All Hope Gone

By this time, Sanders was becoming badly chilled. Even his heavy coat and sleeping bag couldn't keep him warm. He had been out in the **elements** too long. By the end of the third day, parts of his body

Many people enjoy taking vacations in the snowy Alps.

Rescue helicopters searched for Sanders all over the mountain.

had become too cold. He had frostbite on his toes. It hurt too much to walk. He knew that if he tried to go far, he would **collapse**. His only hope was to wait for rescuers to find him.

For two more days, Sanders waited at the cave. At night, he could see the lights from a town five miles away. In the day, he could see people skiing at the nearby ski area. But no one saw him. There was nothing he could do but keep waiting.

Meanwhile, rescuers had given up hope of finding Sanders alive. On December 27 and 28, search helicopters flew all around the mountain. But the wind was still very strong. The helicopters could not get down low enough for rescuers to see well.

By December 29, most of the rescuers thought Sanders was dead. They did not see how anyone could live through such terrible cold for more than three days. But Sanders's mother, Annetta Alms, **insisted** that the rescuers keep looking. So they continued the search for another day.

After that, even Sanders's mother gave up hope. All she wanted then was for rescuers to bring back her son's body. On December 30, they agreed to go out one more time.

Rescued!

That day happened to be Sanders's birthday. By then, he had been trapped on the mountain for six days. He woke up early. The sky was clear. Slowly, he dragged himself up to a nearby **ridge**. He knew that it would be easier for someone to see him from this high and narrow strip of land.

As Sanders sat there, he made a birthday wish. He wished that a helicopter would come. "I knew that was my only hope," he later said.

Then, to his surprise, he got his wish. A helicopter suddenly came right over the top of the ridge. Sanders **signaled** to it. He jumped and waved. "I wasn't about to let them get away," he said.

Rescuers were **shocked** to find Sanders alive. Even his mother couldn't believe it. Doctors treated him for the frostbite on his toes. After his toes healed, he was ready to go to his home near Austin, Texas. For Matt Sanders, his 24th birthday was one he would never forget.

Sanders would never forget his 24th birthday.

Read and Remember — Check the Events

❄ Place a check in front of the three sentences that tell what happened in the story.

_____ **1.** Matt Sanders got lost while looking for his dog.

_____ **2.** Ten people went hiking with Sanders.

_____ **3.** Sanders got caught in a blizzard.

_____ **4.** A sleeping bag helped keep Sanders warm.

_____ **5.** Rescuers thought Sanders was with friends.

_____ **6.** Sanders was found on his birthday.

Write About It

❄ Imagine you are a reporter who talked with Matt Sanders after his rescue. Write a news article warning people of the dangers they face if they go hiking in the Alps.

_____

_____

_____

_____

_____

_____

_____

_____

_____

_____

Focus on Vocabulary — Finish Up

Choose the correct word in dark print to complete each sentence.

elements	**calm**	**signaled**	**shocked**	**mountainside**
insisted	**hike**	**collapse**	**ridge**	**preserve**

1. To walk along a mountain trail is to _____.

2. To fall down is to _____.

3. To be out in wind and snow is to be out in the _____.

4. To have demanded something is to have _____ on it.

5. The side of a mountain is a _____.

6. To be very surprised is to be _____.

7. To keep something safe or protected is to _____ it.

8. Someone who is not nervous or upset is _____.

9. To have motioned or waved to someone is to have _____ to him or her.

10. A high and narrow strip of land is a _____.

Cold Effects on the Body

When a person becomes very cold, his or her body changes to deal with the cold. Some changes, such as **shivering**, help keep the person warm. Shivering is one of the first signs of **hypothermia**. Study the diagram below. Write the answer to each question.

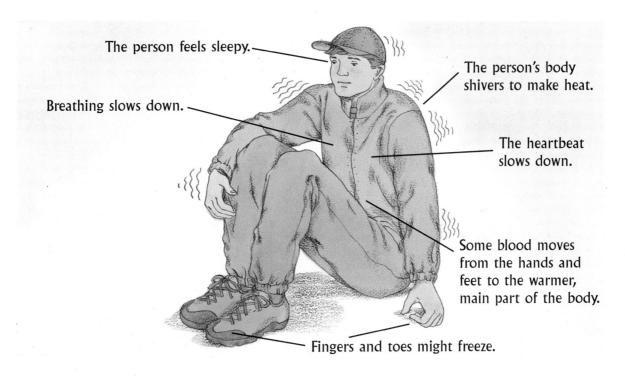

The person feels sleepy.

The person's body shivers to make heat.

Breathing slows down.

The heartbeat slows down.

Some blood moves from the hands and feet to the warmer, main part of the body.

Fingers and toes might freeze.

1. Why does a person's body shiver? _____

2. How does the person's heartbeat change? _____

3. Does the person breathe faster or slower? _____

4. Is the person more likely to feel awake or sleepy? _____

5. In what area does most of the person's blood stay? _____

_____

6. Which is likely to feel colder—the person's hand or belly?

_____

GLOSSARY

✳ Words with this symbol can be found in the SCIENCE CONNECTION.

altitude   page 56
Altitude is height above the sea or another level.

artificial   page 10
Artificial means made by people instead of made by nature.

avalanche   page 9
An avalanche is a huge wall of snow sliding down a hill or mountain.

axis   page 21
✳ The imaginary line that Earth spins on is called an axis.

blizzard   page 7
A blizzard is a bad storm that has thick snow and strong winds.

cables   page 41
Cables are strong thick wires or ropes.

calm   page 95
Calm means quiet and not excited.

cancer   page 87
Cancer is a lump or tumor that grows and spreads in the body.

canvas   page 56
Canvas is a rough, heavy cloth made of cotton or flax.

canyon   page 56
A canyon is a deep valley with tall sloping sides.

capital   page 47
A capital is a place where a government is located.

Celsius   page 69
✳ Celsius is a thermometer scale on which freezing is 0°C and boiling is 100°C.

chilled   page 34
Chilled means made something cold.

cirrus   page 37
✳ Cirrus is a type of white cloud that looks like a small puff, flake, or streak. Cirrus clouds are found very high in the sky.

cliff   page 47
A cliff is a high, tall wall of rock or ice.

climate   pages 87, 93
✳ Climate is the usual weather a place has.

collapse   page 97
Collapse means to fall down.

combination   page 18
A combination is a mixture of things together.

crystals   page 13
✳ Crystals are small pieces of ice. Most ice crystals have six sides.

cumulus   page 37
✳ Cumulus is a type of thick, dense cloud. Cumulus clouds are usually made up of small pieces of ice, water droplets, and sometimes hail. These clouds often bring thunder, lightning, and rain to an area.

fuel   page 88
Fuel is a material that burns and is used to make heat or power.

gust   page 15
A gust is a sudden strong burst of wind.

hail   pages 53
Hail is rounded pieces of ice that sometimes falls during thunderstorms.

hailstones   pages 80, 85
Hailstones are chunks of ice that fall during a storm.

hailstorm   page 80
A hailstorm is a storm in which chunks of ice fall to Earth.

hike   page 95
A hike is a long walk.

hurricane   page 71
A hurricane is a storm that has very strong winds and usually occurs with rain, thunder, and lightning.

hypothermia   pages 49, 101
Hypothermia is when a person's body temperature is very low. People in very cold air or water can be in danger of hypothermia.

incredible   page 8
Incredible means amazing or hard to believe.

injured   page 82
Injured means hurt or damaged.

injuries   page 24
Injuries are hurt areas on a body.

insisted   page 97
Insisted means demanded.

insulation   page 65
Insulation is a material used to help keep out the cold.

isolated   page 87
Isolated means set apart or separated from others.

journey   page 55
A journey is a trip from one place to another.

lungs   page 73
Lungs are parts of the body that help a person breathe air.

map key   page 45
A map key explains what the symbols or colors on a map mean.

meteorologists   page 48
Meteorologists are scientists who study weather.

miracle   page 74
A miracle is an event that cannot be explained by the laws of nature.

moisture   page 81
Moisture means wetness.

mountainside   page 95
The mountainside is the side of a mountain.

narrow   page 47
Narrow means not very wide.

natural disasters   page 72
Natural disasters are terrible events that are caused by nature, such as bad storms or floods.

North Pole   page 23
The North Pole is the point on Earth that is the farthest north.

numb   page 17
Numb means having no feeling.

officials   page 49
Officials are people in charge or in command.

operation   page 90
During an operation, doctors cut into a body to fix a hurt area.

oxygen   page 74
Oxygen is a gas that is found in air. Animals and people need to breathe oxygen to live.

patients   page 40
Patients are sick people who visit doctors or hospitals.

pelted   page 82
Pelted means thrown or hit hard.

physician   page 40
A physician is a doctor who practices medicine.

plow   page 39
Plow means to push or clear away something from the ground.

polar   page 93
Polar is the land area on Earth that is the farthest from the equator. Polar areas are very cold.

precipitation   pages 47, 53
Precipitation is water that falls to Earth in forms, such as rain, snow, and hail.

predicted   page 79
Predicted means guessed or told what was going to happen before it occurred.

preserve   page 96
Preserve means to keep safe or to protect.

protection   page 33
Protection is a defense or something that guards against a danger.

pulse   page 73
A pulse is the regular beating of the blood vessels. It is caused by the beating of the heart.

raged   page 48
Raged means acted out of control.

raindrops   pages 80, 85
Raindrops are drops of rain.

range   pages 55, 61
A range is a row of mountains.

razor   page 72
A razor is a sharp instrument used to shave or cut hair.

remote   page 66
Remote means far away, not easy to get to, or hard to find.

rescue   page 18
Rescue means the act of saving a person who is hurt or in a dangerous place.

research   page 87
Research is information learned by studying a subject.

ridge   page 98
A ridge is a long, narrow part of a mountain.

risky   page 88
Risky means possibly dangerous.

sea level   page 31
Sea level is the average height of the surface of ocean water.

seasons   page 21

Seasons are the four different times of the year when the temperature and amount of sunlight changes. The four seasons are summer, winter, spring, and fall.

shivering   page 17, 101

Shivering means shaking from the cold.

shocked   page 98

Shocked means greatly surprised.

shoveled   page 40

Shoveled means scooped away or moved with a shovel.

signaled   page 98

Signaled means communicated by using a body part or some sound such as a shout.

skylight   page 82

A skylight is a window built into a roof or ceiling.

sleet   page 53

Sleet is small, frozen raindrops.

snowbank   page 15

A snowbank is a mound or hill of snow.

snowdrift   page 15

A snowdrift is a pile of snow formed by the wind.

snowfall   pages 71, 77

Snowfall is the amount of snow that has fallen in a period of time.

snowflake   pag 65

A snowflake is a small crystal of snow.

snowmobile   page 63

A snowmobile is a sled-like machine with a motor.

snowplow   page 40

A snowplow is a machine for clearing away snow.

snowshoeing   page 10

Snowshoeing means walking on snow wearing wooden frames on shoes.

snowstorm   page 32

A snowstorm is a storm with heavy snowfall.

snowsuit   page 63

A snowsuit is a one-piece or two-piece winter suit or clothes.

staggered   page 58

Staggered means walked in a shaky way.

steep   page 56

Steep means almost straight up-and-down or vertical.

stranded   page 48

Stranded means left in a place from which there is no way to leave.

stratus   page 37

Stratus is a type of cloud that has water droplets and sometimes ice. Stratus clouds are not usually very high in the sky.

stunning   page 66

Stunning means very surprising or shocking.

suffered   page 26

Suffered means put up with or felt pain.

survived   page 74

Survived means stayed alive.

Did You Know?

◄ Can you believe that hailstones can be as big as golf balls and even grapefruit? The largest hailstone ever found fell in Kansas in 1970. It was about 17.5 inches around—about the size of a grapefruit. It weighed about 1.7 pounds!

Where was the heaviest ► snowfall ever recorded in North America? About 76 inches of snow fell at Silver Lake, Colorado, in 24 hours in April 1921.

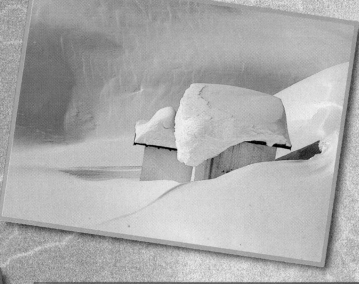

◄ Did you know that ten percent of Earth's land is covered by ice? Thick, large, moving ice and snow is called a glacier. Many glaciers cover land in very cold areas of Earth. If a glacier reaches water, a huge block called an iceberg can break off and float in the water. One iceberg that broke off was as large as the state of Delaware!

◄ Where is the coldest place on Earth? The coldest temperature ever recorded was at the Vostok Station in Antarctica in 1983. It was about –129°F! Antarctica gets much colder than the Arctic. Blizzards in Antarctica can last for weeks.

Do you know how penguins ▶ keep their eggs warm during a blizzard? A male emperor penguin balances an egg on its feet and then covers it with the skin of its belly. This keeps the egg warm even during blizzards in –40°F weather!

◄ Why do some animals' coats change in winter? Animals such as snowshoe hares have brown coats in summer. This helps them hide against dirt, branches, and leaves. In winter, the hares' coats become white to help them hide in the snow. But the arctic fox's coat is white in winter, too, so the hares better be careful!

109

CHART YOUR SCORES

Score Your Work

1. Count the number of correct answers you have for each activity.
2. Write these numbers in the boxes in the chart.
3. Give yourself a score (maximum of 5 points) for **Write About It**.
4. Add up the numbers to get a final score for each tale.
5. Write your final score in the score box.
6. Compare your final score with the maximum score given for each story.

Tales	Read and Remember	Think About It	Write About It	Focus on Vocabulary	Science Connection	Score
Trapped on the Mountain						/24
A Dog to the Rescue						/26
Hero in the Frozen Arctic						/25
Lost in the Cold						/26
The Blizzard of 1996						/23
Stranded on a Narrow Road						/23
Over the Mountains						/24
Twelve Long Days						/25
Buried Under the Snow						/20
Ice from the Sky						/25
Race Against Time						/25
Alone in the Snow						/24

ANSWER KEY

Trapped on the Mountain Pages 6–13

Read and Remember — Choose the Answer:
1. go ice climbing 2. kept climbing up 3. joined the search party 4. in a hole 5. Cam Bradshaw

Think About It — Drawing Conclusions:
Answers will vary. Here are some possible conclusions. 1. They enjoy the challenge. 2. The blinding snow made it very hard to see the trail. 3. They did not think there was any way they could get off the mountain alive. 4. She knew they would lead her to the people in trouble.

Focus on Vocabulary — Find the Meaning:
1. bad snowstorm 2. thick, blowing snow 3. walked away from 4. level of heat 5. how cold the air feels 6. amazing 7. rushing snow 8. walking on snow with special shoes 9. harm 10. made by people

Science Connection — How Snow Forms:
1. water vapor 2. Ice crystals can form. 3. six 4. Flakes of snow are made when ice crystals stick together. 5. 32°F or colder

A Dog to the Rescue Pages 14–21

Read and Remember — Finish the Sentence:
1. play outside 2. wind 3. a fence 4. snow 5. neck 6. house

Write About It: Answers will vary.

Focus on Vocabulary — Match Up:
1. distance something can be seen 2. sudden burst of wind 3. hill of snow 4. pile of snow made by wind 5. shaking 6. without feeling 7. very tired 8. went out of sight 9. mixture 10. act of saving someone

Science Connection — Seasons:
1. winter, spring, summer, fall 2. an imaginary line on which Earth spins 3. summer 4. winter 5. spring

Hero in the Frozen Arctic Pages 22–29

Read and Remember – Check the Events:
2, 3, 5

Think About It – Fact or Opinion:
1. F 2. O 3. F 4. F 5. F 6. O 7. F 8. O

Focus on Vocabulary – Crossword Puzzle:
ACROSS — 3. frostbite 6. degrees 8. injuries

9. deserts 10. suffered DOWN — 1. efforts 2. North Pole 4. tundra 5. debris 7. survivors

Science Connection — Wind-Chill Chart:
1. miles per hour 2. same as actual air temperature 3. 3°F 4. –53°F

Lost in the Cold Pages 30–37

Read and Remember — Choose the Answer:
1. They ran out of gas. 2. a small amount of gas 3. They got lost. 4. two hunters 5. She stayed in the van. 6. two weeks

Write About It: Answers will vary.

Focus on Vocabulary — Finish the Pargraphs:
1. forecast 2. snowstorm 3. elevation 4. sea level 5. wilderness 6. frosty 7. directions 8. protection 9. chilled 10. exposure

Science Connection — Cloud Types:
1. cirrus 2. stratus 3. cirrus 4. big and puffy 5. below 6,000 feet

The Blizzard of 1996 Pages 38–45

Read and Remember — Finish the Sentence:
1. into the East River 2. He walked. 3. on skis 4. blowing snow 5. They closed. 6. one hundred

Think About It — Find the Main Idea:
3, 4

Focus on Vocabulary — Finish Up:
1. physician 2. snowplow 3. transportation 4. velocity 5. flurries 6. plow 7. emergencies 8. patients 9. cables 10. shoveled

Science Connection — Weather Map:
1. ☼ 2. light blue 3. rainy 4. Minneapolis 5. New York City

Stranded on a Narrow Road Pages 46–53

Read and Remember — Check the Events:
1, 3, 6

Write About It: Answers will vary.

Focus on Vocabulary -– Make a Word:
1. hypothermia 2. raged 3. cliff 4. precipitation 5. officials 6. meteorologists 7. capital 8. stranded 9. travelers 10. narrow. The letters in the circles spell *helicopter*.

Science Connection — Kinds of Precipitation:
1. join together 2. snow 3. freezing 4. air 5. sleet

Over the Mountains Pages 54–61

Read and Remember — Choose the Answer:
1. Himalayas 2. Chinese leaders 3. a blanket and coat 4. in the snow 5. his girlfriend

Think About It — Cause and Effect:
1. c 2. a 3. d 4. b

Focus on Vocabulary — Finish the Paragraphs:
1. journey 2. range 3. altitude 4. staggered 5. customs 6. endure 7. windbreakers 8. canyon 9. canvas 10. steep

Science Connection — Mountain Heights:
1. 29,028 feet 2. Aconcagua 3. Africa 4. Mount McKinley 5. Australia

Twelve Long Days Pages 62–69

Read and Remember — Finish the Sentence:
1. dogs 2. hotel 3. snow 4. dropped 5. dogs barking

Write About It: Answers will vary.

Focus on Vocabulary — Crossword Puzzle:
ACROSS — 3. teeny 4. whim 5. insulation 7. stunning 9. snowmobile DOWN —1. snowsuit 2. Fahrenheit 3. terriers 6. snowflake 8. remote

Science Connection — Thermometers:
1. 0°C 2. a person's body 3. Celsius 4. 32°F 5. 32°F

Buried Under the Snow Pages 70–77

Read and Remember — Check the Events:
1, 2, 3

Think About It — Find the Main Ideas:
2, 4

Focus on Vocabulary — Find the Meaning:
1. the amount of snow 2. storm with strong winds 3. shaving tool 4. terrible events in nature 5. not believing 6. regular beating in blood vessels 7. parts of the body used for breathing 8. something amazing 9. lived 10. gas in air

Science Connection — Snowfall Amounts:
1. May 2. 5 3. January 4. August 5. winter

Ice from the Sky Pages 78–85

Read and Remember — Choose the Answer:
1. clear 2. He called the airport. 3. large chunks of ice 4. in her home 5. a few minutes

Write About It: Answers will vary.

Focus on Vocabulary — Match Up:
1. person reporting the weather 2. told ahead of time 3. formed 4. chunks of ice 5. storm with hail 6. drops of rain 7. wetness 8. window in a roof 9. hurt 10. hit hard

Science Connection — How Hail Forms:
1. A water droplet is blown high in the cloud. 2. The water freezes. 3. Freezing line 4. The ice drops and collects more water, which freezes on it. 5. when it becomes too heavy

Race Against Time Pages 86–93

Read and Remember — Finish the Sentence:
1. Antarctica 2. medicine 3. sunshine 4. freeze 5. flown home

Think About It — Find the Sequence:
1. 2 2. 1 3. 5 4. 3 5. 4

Focus on Vocabulary — Make a Word:
1. climate 2. cancer 3. research 4. fuel 5. isolated 6. risky 7. windstorms 8. expert 9. exploded 10. operation. The letters in the circles spell *McAllister*.

Science Connection — Climate Areas:
1. polar, temperate, tropical 2. tropical 3. polar 4. mild, with warm summers and cold winters 5. warm

Alone in the Snow Pages 94–101

Read and Remember — Check the Events:
3, 4, 6

Write About It: Answers will vary.

Focus on Vocabulary — Finish Up:
1. hike 2. collapse 3. elements 4. insisted 5. mountainside 6. shocked 7. preserve 8. calm 9. signaled 10. ridge

Science Connection — Cold Effects on the Body:
1. to make heat 2. It slows down. 3. slower 4. sleepy 5. main part of the body 6. the person's hand